THE
TIMES
BOOK
OF
VEGETARIAN
COOKERY

THE TIMES BOOK OF VEGETARIAN COOKERY

Frances Bissell

Chatto & Windus

LONDON

First published in 1994 by
Chatto & Windus Limited
Random House, 20 Vauxhall Bridge Road, London SW1V 2SA

1 3 5 7 9 10 8 6 4 2

Random House Australia (Pty) Limited
20 Alfred Street, Milsons Point, Sydney,
New South Wales 2061, Australia

Random House New Zealand Limited
18 Poland Road, Glenfield
Auckland 10, New Zealand

Random House South Africa (Pty) Limited
PO Box 337, Bergvlei, South Africa

Random House UK Limited Reg. No. 954009

A CIP catalogue record for this book
is available from the British Library

ISBN 0 7011 6202 3

Typeset in Simoncini Garamond by
SX Composing Limited, Rayleigh, Essex
Printed in Great Britain by
Butler & Tanner Ltd, Frome, Somerset

CONTENTS

Introduction 7

Soups and Starters 9

Light Meals and Snacks 35

Salads and Side Dishes 59

Main Dishes 87

Desserts and Baking 137

Entertaining 163

Index 168

Introduction

Today, an increasing number of people prefer to eat a vegetarian diet, for a wide range of reasons. Vegetarian food has much to offer. It is generally economical and nutritious, and provides delicious, appetizing meals that are quick and easy to prepare, a valuable addition to any cook's repertoire.

This book caters for the majority of vegetarians who do not eat anything derived from the slaughter of animals or fish, but who do eat eggs (free-range) and dairy produce.

The following chapters contain innovative recipe ideas which should inspire and add variety to any diet. The chapters are arranged by course, each chapter dealing with a particular component of a meal, but the recipes are incredibly versatile. Many of the soups, for example, served with warm crusty bread, would make a delicious meal on their own. The chapters are designed to make meal-planning easy, but should not stop you from adapting recipes to suit your own requirements.

A NOTE ON INGREDIENTS

Butter

Many of the recipes in this book use butter as an ingredient. Vegetable margarine can be used as an alternative, if preferred, but remember to read the labels of margarine tubs and packets carefully (or to look for a 'suitable-for-vegetarians' symbol) as some margarines contain fish oils or rennet containing whey.

Cheese

Many types of cheese are made using animal rennet, but vegetarians generally insist on using only cheeses made with non-animal rennet. Many supermarkets and delicatessens stock vegetarian cheeses and these can be used in any of the recipes in this book. If you cannot find a vegetarian version of a particular cheese, use one that is similar; for example, Sapsago or Sbrinz can be used instead of Parmesan. Many brands of fresh, soft or cream cheeses are vegetarian, as are Italian mozzarella and Greek feta cheeses. (Vegans can use soya cheese in cooking.)

Eggs

Eggs are one of the cook's most valuable ingredients. Highly nutritious, yet relatively inexpensive, they are easy to cook and supremely versatile. Always use free-range eggs, of course, which, even putting aside the moral issue, taste much better than battery-produced eggs.

Flour

Wholemeal flour is specified in many of the recipes in this book, and can be used in the others in place of white, if preferred.

Pulses

The family of dried beans and peas, known as pulses, when cooked alone, have an agreeable but sometimes rather bland flavour, but this makes them ideal companions to stronger flavours.

In order for dried beans to become edible, their moisture content must be restored by allowing them to absorb as much water as possible. Six hours soaking will usually be adequate, except for chick peas and soya beans which may need longer, but lentils need little or no soaking. On the other hand, if it is more convenient to do so, overnight soaking shortens the cooking time. Soaking in warm water is a quick way of getting beans to the cooking stage. Another way is to pour plenty of boiling water over the beans and to let them soak for 2 hours, by which time the water will be cold. Even more effective is to bring them slowly to the boil, then allow to cool in the water. There are also those who advocate long slow cooking of beans and those who favour the pressure cooker. There is no right or wrong way. It depends on the dish, the bean and your preferred method. However, kidney beans, both red and black, should be boiled for 15 minutes after soaking. The beans are then drained and rinsed before final cooking. Toxins are present on the skin of kidney beans, and these are rendered harmless by boiling.

Beans and peas make excellent purées, soups and vegetable accompaniments, as well as adding colour to salads.

Soups and Starters

Received wisdom has it that in order to make soup, you need to start with a good, flavoursome, homemade stock, and, for vegetable soups in particular, this is almost always the case. Homemade stock adds an extra depth of flavour that cannot always be achieved with water alone when making soups from delicately flavoured vegetables such as lettuce, say, or peas. In some soups, however, extra flavour comes from the judicious addition of a few herbs or spices, providing, for instance, a counterbalance to the starchy sweetness of root vegetables, and in some soups, such as the Fresh Tomato Soup on page 18, the flavour comes simply from fresh, sweet, ripe tomatoes.

The recipe for Vegetable Broth (see opposite) can be used as a base for the soups in this chapter. If you want to make a stock-based soup but have no pre-prepared stock and no time to make it, there are some good instant substitutes available that are free of artificial flavour enhancers, gluten and lactose, as well as artificial colouring and preservatives.

Soups are wonderful standbys. They can be made ahead, frozen and used when needed. Substantial soups, full of chunky vegetables, pulses and pasta, need no more than warm bread rolls or crusty French bread to accompany them and can form the main course of a meal. Lighter soups double up as simple starters: a delicately flavoured, chilled Carrot and Peach Soup (see page 24), for example, is the ideal first course for a patio lunch on a hot summer's day.

This chapter includes both hot and cold starters, ranging from the more elegant dinner-party starters like Vegetable and Tofu Creams (see page 29), for example, to the simple informal Poached and Marinated Vegetables (see page 30) which can be made ahead and then chilled until needed.

Vegetable Broth

Makes 3 pt / 1.70 l

This recipe can be used as a base for all the soups in this chapter, and indeed for some of the vegetable, rice and grain recipes in other chapters. It also makes an excellent lunchtime snack.

1 tsp olive oil
1 onion, peeled and finely chopped
1 carrot, peeled and thinly sliced
2 celery stalks, trimmed and sliced
1 leek, trimmed and sliced
8 oz / 230 g tomatoes, peeled and
　chopped
6 parsley stalks

6 watercress stalks
1 oz / 30 g lentils
1 oz / 30 g dried beans
1 oz / 30 g chick peas
4 pt / 2.30 l water
salt
freshly ground black pepper

Heat the olive oil in a large saucepan. Add the onion and fry gently until it begins to brown and caramelize. This will give the broth a good colour. Add the rest of the vegetables, the parsley and watercress. Rinse the lentils, beans and chick peas, and add to the saucepan together with 3 pt / 1.70 l water and salt and pepper to taste. Bring to the boil, and simmer for 2–3 hours, partially covered. Strain into a bowl. Return the debris to the pan with 1 pt / 570 ml water. Bring to the boil and cook for 15 minutes, then strain into the rest of the broth, pressing down well on the debris in the sieve. Cool and chill until required.

Pea and Herb Soup

Serves 6

½ oz / 15 g butter *or* 1 tbsp
  sunflower oil
2 shallots *or* 1 small onion, peeled
  and chopped
1 celery stalk, trimmed and
  chopped
8 oz / 230 g pea pods, chopped
  (optional)
1 small lettuce, chopped
1 small cucumber, chopped

3–4 oz / 85–110 g potatoes, peeled and
  diced
2 pt / 1.15 l vegetable stock
handful of any of the following: parsley,
  chervil, purslane, rocket, basil,
  watercress, chopped
6 oz / 170 g fresh peas
salt
freshly ground black pepper
cream *(optional)*

Heat the butter or oil in a large saucepan, and gently fry the shallots or onion without browning. Add the celery, pea pods (if using), lettuce, cucumber, potatoes and stock. Bring to the boil, and simmer until the celery and potatoes are tender. Add half the herbs, and cook for a few minutes more. Make a purée of the soup in a blender or food processor, and sieve into a clean saucepan. Add the fresh peas and the remaining herbs, and cook until the peas are tender. Season to taste just before serving, and stir in cream if desired.

Asparagus Soup

Serves 4

*This is a good recipe for using up the tougher ends of the stalks or a
bundle of mixed asparagus of different sizes. It can be served hot
or chilled.*

1 lb / 455 g asparagus
2 shallots
½ tbsp olive oil, if serving the soup
  chilled *or* ½ oz / 15 g butter, if
  serving it hot
1½ pt / 850 ml vegetable stock
1 tsp marjoram leaves

salt
freshly ground black pepper
2 ripe tomatoes, peeled, deseeded and
  chopped
1 tbsp balsamic or sherry vinegar
1 tbsp single cream
chives, to garnish

Wash the asparagus thoroughly, chop off the ends, and peel off any coarse outer skin with a potato peeler. Cut off and reserve the four best-looking tips for garnishing, and cut the rest into 1 in / 2.5 cm chunks. Peel and chop the shallots, and sweat in the oil or butter in a large saucepan. Add the asparagus, the vegetable stock and the marjoram. Bring to the boil, lower the heat, and simmer gently until the asparagus is tender. Allow the soup to cool slightly, and then blend it in a food blender or processor. Sieve it, and either return to the pan if serving it hot, or cool and then chill it. Season to taste.

Make a purée of the raw tomatoes, sieve them, and stir in the vinegar. Quickly steam or boil the reserved asparagus tips. Pour the soup into bowls, hot or chilled, as desired. Carefully spoon a swirl of the tomato vinaigrette and a swirl of cream into each bowl, and garnish with the chives, chopped or left long, and with the asparagus tips.

Aubergine, Corn and Tomato Soup

Serves 6–8

This soup is based on one served at Colettes, an unexpected haven for simple home-cooking on Wilshire Boulevard in Beverly Hills.

1 medium onion	2–3 corn cobs
1 aubergine, about 12 oz / 340 g	salt
6 firm ripe tomatoes, peeled, deseeded and chopped	freshly ground black pepper
	1–2 tbsp finely chopped parsley
2½ pt / 1.45 l vegetable stock	

Peel and finely chop the onion. Slice and then dice the aubergine into about ½ in / 1 cm cubes. 'Fry' the onion and aubergine in a large non-stick pan until soft and wilted and beginning to brown a little. Add the tomatoes and stock, and continue cooking until the flavour has begun to develop. Husk the corn cobs, and cut the kernels from the cobs by standing each one vertically on a chopping board and slicing down with a sharp knife, cutting off as much of the flesh as possible. Add the corn kernels to the soup, together with salt and pepper to taste. Bring to the boil, and simmer for a few minutes, until the corn is just tender. Stir in the chopped parsley and serve.

The flavour of the soup can be heightened with a dash of lemon juice, balsamic vinegar or fino sherry. Extra body can be added to the soup by putting a handful or so of rice in the pan when you have first brought the stock to the boil.

Spiced Carrot and Parsnip Soup

Serves 4–6

The idea of making the two main ingredients into two separate soups, and then pouring them into the soup bowl so that they swirl together in a pattern, keeping their colours distinct, comes from Alice Waters' restaurant in Berkeley, Chez Panisse, where her chef, Paul Bertolli, is, in her words, 'very strong on soups'. It looks and tastes very good, and is only a little more trouble to make than combining all the ingredients together, which of course, you can do for a more homely dish. Either way, inexpensive and humble ingredients are transformed into a delicious soup.

½ oz / 15 g unsalted butter
1 medium onion, peeled and sliced

1 celery stalk, trimmed and thinly sliced

Carrot soup
8 oz / 230 g carrots, peeled and thinly sliced
¼ tsp ground cardamom
¾ pt / 430 ml vegetable stock
¼ pt / 140 ml full-cream milk or single cream
salt
freshly ground black pepper

Parsnip soup
8 oz / 230 g parsnips, peeled and thinly sliced
¼ tsp freshly grated nutmeg
¾ pt / 430 ml vegetable stock
¼ pt / 140 ml full-cream milk or single cream
salt
freshly ground black pepper

Use two saucepans. Melt half the butter in each. Divide the onion and celery between the two pans and gently sweat them in the butter. Add the carrots and cardamom to one pan and the parsnips and nutmeg to the other. Cook for 2–3 minutes, and then pour on the stock, ¾ pt / 430 ml into each pan. Cover and let it simmer gently for 15–20 minutes or until the vegetables are tender. Allow to cool slightly.

Blend the parsnip mixture with ¼ pt / 140 ml milk or cream in a blender or food processor, sieve it, and pour it back into a clean saucepan. Rinse the blender goblet or food processor bowl, and blend the carrot mixture in the same way. Reheat the two soups, season to taste, pour some of each into heated soup bowls, and swirl together gently to form a pattern. For a denser, chewier texture, serve the soup without sieving it.

Black Bean Soup

One of our very favourite winter soups.

8 oz / 230 g black kidney beans
1 medium onion
1 tbsp sunflower or olive oil
1 tbsp ground cumin
1 tbsp paprika
¼ tsp cayenne pepper or chilli
  powder
3 cloves *or* ¼ tsp ground cloves

1 tbsp tomato purée
1 pt / 570 ml stock or water
salt
4–6 tbsp good dry or medium sherry
  (optional)
4–6 thin slices of lemon
1 tbsp finely chopped parsley
4–6 tbsp soured cream *(optional)*

Soak the beans in cold water overnight. Next day, drain and rinse them, place them in a saucepan and cover with at least 2 in / 5 cm water. Boil for 15 minutes. Drain and return them to the pan with fresh water. Bring slowly to the boil, cover and barely simmer for 2–2½ hours, until the beans are tender.

Meanwhile, peel and finely chop the onion, and fry it in the oil in a heavy saucepan until beginning to brown. Add the cumin, paprika, cayenne pepper or chilli and cloves, and cook for 2–3 minutes. Stir in the tomato purée, and cook until the mixture thickens and darkens as the water evaporates. Pour on half the stock or water, bring to the boil, cover and simmer for 30 minutes or until the onions are soft.

Allow the cooked beans to cool slightly in their liquid before making a purée of them in a food processor or blender. It is best to do this in two batches, unless you have a large-capacity machine. Add the bean purée to the onion and spice mixture, together with the rest of the stock or water. Stir until thoroughly mixed, bring to the boil, and add salt to taste. If the consistency is too thick for you, gradually add a little more water or stock and appropriate seasoning, until the taste and consistency are as you want them.

There are several ways of serving this soup – with or without sherry, a thin slice of hard-boiled egg, or a thin slice of lemon, in any combination. I like to serve the soup very hot, pouring it when practically boiling into earthenware soup bowls containing a splash of sherry (or, even better, rum) so that the heat of the soup evaporates most of the alcohol, leaving the spirity flavour behind. I then add to each bowl a very thin slice of lemon, a sprinkling of finely chopped parsley and perhaps a tablespoonful of soured cream.

Asparagus and Almond Soup

Serves 4–6

12 oz / 340 g asparagus
2 shallots, peeled and chopped
2 garlic cloves, peeled and chopped
½ celery stalk, trimmed and sliced
1 tbsp sunflower oil

2 pt / 1.15 l vegetable stock
2 oz / 60 g ground almonds
salt
freshly ground black pepper
1 oz / 30 g toasted flaked almonds

Wash the asparagus and cut off any very woody bits. Chop the rest. Sweat all the vegetables in the oil for 5–10 minutes without browning, and then pour on all but ¼ pt / 140 ml of the stock. Bring to the boil, and simmer until the vegetables are tender. Purée in a blender or food processor, then sieve into a saucepan. Meanwhile, put the ground almonds in a small frying pan, and stir over a moderate heat. This is not to brown them but just to bring out their flavour. Blend in the remaining stock and stir to a smooth paste. Mix this into the soup. Bring to the boil and season to taste. Serve, scattering toasted almond flakes on the soup in each bowl.

Cream of Spinach Soup

Serves 4

This simple soup recipe can be adapted to many vegetables – broccoli, lettuce, chard, watercress, sorrel and cauliflower (add a pinch of curry powder), for example. Add potato during cooking for a thicker soup.

1 small onion or shallot, peeled and
  finely chopped
½ oz / 15 g butter, if serving hot *or*
  ½ tbsp olive oil, if serving cold
1½ lb / 680 g spinach, washed and
  drained

1¼ pt / 710 ml vegetable stock
¼ pt / 140 ml whipping cream
salt
freshly ground black pepper
freshly grated nutmeg

In a large saucepan, sweat the onion or shallot in the butter or oil until soft and translucent. Stir in the spinach. As it wilts, it will gradually lose its volume. Pour on half the stock, and cook for approximately 4–5 minutes or until the spinach is just tender.

Allow to cool slightly, and place in a blender or food processor. Pour on half the remaining stock, and blend until smooth. It can be sieved or not, as you wish (this may depend on whether the spinach was very stalky or not). Stir in the cream and the rest of the stock. Season to taste with salt, pepper and nutmeg, then bring to the boil and serve, or chill until required.

Pumpkin and Almond Soup

Serves 4–6

This is from Italian friends, based on a Renaissance recipe, with delicate, subtle flavours and almonds to thicken it.

2 lb / 900 g piece of butternut squash or pumpkin	1½ pt / 850 ml vegetable stock
2 shallots	salt
1 tbsp grapeseed or almond oil	freshly ground black pepper
4 oz / 110 g blanched almonds	freshly grated nutmeg
juice and grated zest of 1 orange	2–3 oz /60–85 g Parmesan cheese, freshly grated

Remove the seeds and filaments from the squash or pumpkin and bake in the oven at 180°C / 350°F / Mark 4 in a roasting tin until tender. Meanwhile, peel and chop the shallots, and sweat in the oil in a large saucepan until transparent. Chop the almonds finely and stir into the shallots. Add the baked pumpkin flesh together with the orange juice and zest and ½ pt / 280 ml stock. Cook for 5 minutes or until the shallots are tender, and then make a purée in a blender or food processor. Return to the saucepan with the rest of the stock and reheat. Season to taste with salt, pepper and nutmeg (for me, nutmeg and pumpkin go together like rhubarb and ginger or apple and cinnamon, and I tend to use a lot of it). Just before serving this thick soup in small heated soup bowls or plates, stir in the Parmesan so that it will have melted into the soup by the time you eat it.

Fresh Tomato Soup with Quenelles

Serves 4

Use the tastiest, ripest, sweetest tomatoes you can find.

1½ lb / 680 g ripe tomatoes
1 oz / 30 g chilled butter, cut into
  cubes
1 tbsp, or more if you like, finely
  shredded basil

salt
freshly ground black pepper

Peel and deseed the tomatoes in a sieve over a basin to catch the juices. Cut the tomatoes into very thin, short slivers, and place in a heavy saucepan with the sieved juice. Heat gently until the tomatoes begin to 'sweat' and give off their liquid. Stir in the cubes of butter, one at a time, so that each blends with the tomato before adding the next. Stir in the basil, season to taste, and serve immediately. It should still have a very fresh, uncooked flavour.

At Leith's, where I first tasted it, this soup is served with basil-flavoured cream cheese quenelles (see below). These are quite tricky, and the mixture should be made the day before. If you do not have time, mix some finely chopped basil into seasoned cream cheese, and place a spoonful in each bowl of soup as you serve it.

Quenelles

Serves 4

1 oz / 30 g butter
2 egg yolks
1½ oz / 40 g soft white
  breadcrumbs

3½ oz / 100 g cream cheese
1 tbsp finely chopped basil

Beat the butter and egg yolks together until smooth. Add the rest of the ingredients, and allow the mixture to rest overnight. Form into small dumplings or sausages, and slide them gently into a large pan of water, held just at the boil. When they float to the surface, they are cooked, and should be removed with a slotted spoon and served immediately with the hot soup.

Minestrone

4 oz / 110 g dried haricot or
  cannellini beans, soaked overnight
  and drained
4 oz / 110 g dried flageolet beans,
  soaked overnight and drained
2 tbsp extra virgin olive oil
1 onion, peeled and chopped
1 leek, trimmed and finely sliced
2 carrots, peeled and chopped
2 celery stalks, trimmed and finely
  sliced
1 small turnip, peeled and chopped
12 oz / 340 g cabbage
6 oz / 170 g green beans
14 oz / 400 g can plum tomatoes,
  roughly chopped

½ pt / 280 ml dry white wine
1½ pt / 850 ml vegetable stock
1 bay leaf
sprig of thyme
salt
freshly ground black pepper
8 oz / 230 g pasta shapes, broken
  spaghetti or macaroni
2 tbsp pesto
Accompaniments
freshly grated hard cheese
thick slices of lightly toasted wholemeal
  bread

Put the beans in a saucepan, cover with water, bring to the boil, and simmer until tender. This may take 2–3 hours, depending on the age of the beans. Heat the oil in a flameproof casserole. Add the onion, leek, carrots, celery and turnip, and fry until the onion is transparent.

Wash and trim the cabbage. Cut out and discard the hard core. Shred the cabbage and put it to one side. Top and tail the green beans, and break them in two if necessary. Put with the cabbage.

Add the tomatoes, white wine, ½ pt / 280 ml stock and the herbs to the casserole. Simmer until the vegetables are soft. Once the dried beans are almost tender, mix them with the vegetables, together with their cooking liquor. Add the rest of the stock, season lightly, and bring to the boil. Add the pasta, cabbage and green beans. Cook for a further 10–15 minutes. Stir in the pesto and serve. Hand the cheese and bread separately.

Vegetable Gumbo

Serves 6–8

This is more of a meal than a soup. There are enough vegetables to stand a spoon up in it, and the okra thickens the broth to a silky-rich texture. You can vary the other vegetables according to what is available.

1 large onion, peeled and chopped
4 ripe tomatoes, peeled, deseeded and chopped
3 celery stalks, trimmed and thinly sliced
2 tbsp olive oil
4 oz / 110 g okra, trimmed and sliced
1 red or green pepper, deseeded and sliced
3 pt / 1.70 l vegetable stock

8 oz / 230 g bobby beans, trimmed
8 oz / 230 g courgettes, thickly sliced
kernels of 2–3 corn cobs *or* 6 oz / 170 g baby corn
8 oz / 230 g chick peas or black-eyed beans, soaked and cooked, plus their cooking liquid
sprigs of coriander, thyme, parsley and bay leaves
salt
freshly ground black pepper
finely chopped parsley or coriander

Fry the onion, tomatoes and celery in the oil until the onion and celery are translucent and the tomatoes collapsed. Add the sliced okra and pepper, together with the stock. Bring to the boil, and simmer for 20–30 minutes. Add the rest of the vegetables, the chick peas or black-eyed beans and their cooking liquid, and the herbs (tied together). Continue cooking until the vegetables are done to your liking. Remove the bundle of herbs, season the soup, and stir in the chopped parsley or coriander before serving. You might like to add a dash of hot pepper sauce.

Dried Tomato and Garlic Soup

Serves 4–6

4 oz / 110 g sun-dried tomatoes
1 pt / 570 ml boiling water
2 shallots *or* 1 small onion
6–8 garlic cloves
1 tbsp extra virgin olive oil

1 bay leaf
pinch of dried thyme
1 pt / 570 ml vegetable stock
salt
freshly ground black pepper

Chop the tomatoes and cover them with the boiling water. Leave them to soften while you peel the shallots or onion and the garlic and sweat them in the olive oil until soft. Add the tomatoes with their soaking liquid, and the herbs. Simmer for 5–8 minutes or until the vegetables are tender. Put in a blender or food processor with the stock, and blend until smooth. Sieve if you wish. Bring back to the boil, and season to taste. A splash of sherry is very good in this. If you have a can of borlotti or cannellini beans, these will stretch the soup as well as turn it into something much more substantial.

Beetroot and Tomato Soup

Serves 4

1 tbsp olive oil
1 onion, peeled and finely chopped
1 celery stalk, trimmed and finely
 chopped
1 small carrot, peeled and finely
 chopped
3 garlic cloves, peeled and crushed
1 tbsp dill seed or chopped fresh dill

14 oz / 400 g can plum tomatoes
8 oz / 230 g cooked (but not pickled)
 beetroot, peeled and diced
1½ pt / 850 ml vegetable stock
To serve (optional)
2–3 tbsp soured cream
fresh dill

Heat the olive oil in a heavy saucepan and sweat the onion, celery and carrot for 20–30 minutes without browning. Add the garlic and dill, and cook for 2–3 minutes more. Add the tomatoes, and cook on a high heat until much of their juice has evaporated. Put in the beetroot and the stock, bring to the boil, and simmer for 15–20 minutes. Rub through a sieve into a clean saucepan and bring to the boil, then serve immediately. Spoon a little cream into each soup bowl, if liked, and garnish with fronds of fresh dill, if available.

Watercress Soup

Serves 6

2 onions, peeled and thinly sliced
1 tbsp grapeseed oil
½ oz / 15 g butter
8 oz / 230 g (2–3 bunches)
  watercress, trimmed
3 pt / 1.70 l vegetable stock

1 lb / 455 g potatoes, peeled and diced
¼ pt / 140 ml crème fraîche or single
  cream
salt
freshly ground black pepper

Sweat the onions in the oil and butter in a saucepan. Rinse and roughly chop the watercress, and stir into the onions. Cook until the watercress has wilted, then add the stock and potatoes. Simmer for about 30 minutes or until the potatoes are soft. Sieve or purée in a blender or food processor until smooth, and then return the soup to the saucepan. Stir in the cream, season, and bring back to the boil. Serve with croûtons, if you like, or slices of baguette or triangles of bread spread with butter and crisped in the oven.

Onion and Cheese Soup under a Soufflé

Serves 6

1 lb / 455 g onions, peeled and
  chopped
½ pt / 280 ml vegetable stock
2 pt / 1.15 l milk
3 oz / 85 g butter
3 oz / 85 g plain flour

12 oz / 340 g farmhouse Lancashire
  cheese, grated
salt
freshly ground black pepper
freshly grated nutmeg
3 eggs, separated

Using a non-stick pan, sweat the onion until transparent and just beginning to caramelize, but do not burn. Add the stock, and cook until the onion is soft.

Meanwhile, pre-heat the oven to 200°C / 400°F / Mark 6, bring the milk to the boil and, in another saucepan melt the butter. Stir the flour into the butter, and cook for 5 minutes. Slowly add ¼ pt / 140 ml boiled milk, whisking it to prevent any lumps forming. Stir in the cheese until melted. Set aside 3 tablespoons of this roux mixture, and add the remaining milk to the roux remaining in the pan, stirring continuously. Add the onion and stock and mix well. Bring to the boil, and add salt, pepper and nutmeg to taste.

Divide the mixture between six ovenproof soup bowls placed on a baking sheet. Beat the egg yolks into the roux that you have set aside, whisk the whites to firm peaks, and gently fold the two together. Spoon this soufflé mixture on top of the soup bowls, and bake in the preheated oven for 10–12 minutes. Serve at once.

Onion Soup

Serves 4

2 large Spanish onions
1 tbsp olive or sunflower oil
1¼ pt / 710 ml vegetable stock
salt

freshly ground black pepper
4 slices of French bread
4 tbsp grated cheese, such as Gruyère or
  Comté

Peel the onions and slice them very very thinly with a sharp knife. (It is better to do this by hand as the slicing disc of a food processor, although efficient, has a tendency to force liquid out of the onions, making them more inclined to steam than fry.) Heat the oil in a large frying pan, and fry the onions, stirring continuously. The secret here is to get the onions as brown as possible without burning them. The browning is the result of caramelizing the natural sugar present in the onion, and is what gives the soup its colour and flavour. (This is why I use a frying pan instead of a saucepan at this stage.) Once the onion is thoroughly browned, scrape it into a saucepan and pour on the stock. Bring to the boil and simmer until the onion is tender. Season to taste. Toast the bread slices on one side only and sprinkle the cheese on the untoasted side. Pour the soup into four ovenproof soup bowls, float the cheese bread on top and finish off under the grill or in the top of a hot oven. Serve when the cheese has melted and is bubbling.

Carrot and Peach Soup

Serves 4

This chilled soup has a wonderfully soothing quality, both in its delicate colour and its velvety texture. The peach flavour is barely there, but just enough to intrigue.

2 shallots, peeled and finely sliced
8 oz / 230 g carrots, peeled and
   thinly sliced
1¼ pt / 710 ml vegetable stock
1 large or 2 small ripe peaches

good pinch of ground cardamom
salt
freshly ground white pepper
2–3 tbsp yoghurt or single cream
   (*optional*)

Put the shallots and carrots in a saucepan with a quarter of the stock. Cook until soft. Cool slightly. Stone the peach(es), roughly chop the fruit and place in a food processor or blender with the carrot and shallot mixture. Add a little more stock and the cardamom. Process until smooth. Sieve and mix with the rest of the stock. Cool rapidly, and chill until ready to serve. Season to taste just before serving. If you want to enrich it, also stir in the yoghurt or cream just before serving.

Variation ∾ Substitute mango for the peach, and before cooking the vegetables in the stock, fry them in sunflower oil with the cardamom and a teaspoon of ground cumin until the shallots are golden brown.

Summer Vichyssoise

Serves 4–6

1 medium potato, peeled and
   chopped
1 onion, peeled and chopped
1 tbsp sunflower oil
1½ lb / 680 g green vegetables, such
   as fennel, celery, courgettes, peas,
   asparagus, broad beans

2 pt / 1.15 l vegetable stock
handful of fresh herbs, such as parsley,
   chives, chervil and sorrel
salt
freshly ground black pepper
3–4 tbsp yoghurt or single cream
   (*optional*)

Fry the potato and onion gently in the oil for a few minutes without browning. Wash, trim and roughly chop the green vegetables as appropriate. Any tough ones, such as fennel or celery, should be put on to cook at this stage. Add about ¼ pt / 140 ml stock, and cook until the vegetables are soft. Add the rest of the greens and half the herbs, and cook until the greens are done. Allow to cool slightly, make a purée in a blender or food processor, sieve, and stir in the rest of the stock. Finely chop the remaining herbs, and stir these in. Chill until ready to serve. Just before serving, season to taste, and, if using, stir in the yoghurt or single cream.

Chilled Courgette and Potato Soup

Serves 4

1 medium onion, peeled and finely chopped
2 tbsp sunflower oil
12 oz / 340 g courgettes, trimmed and diced
1 medium potato, peeled and diced

1½ pt / 850 ml vegetable stock
handful of fresh basil
salt
freshly ground white pepper
¼ pt / 140 ml single cream

Sweat the onion in the oil in a large saucepan until soft. Add the courgettes and potato to the saucepan, pour on half the stock, bring to the boil, and simmer until the vegetables are tender. Put most of the basil, leaves and stalks, in a blender or food processor, keeping a little for garnish. Pour on the vegetables, and process until smooth. Sieve if necessary, season lightly, stir in the remaining stock and the cream, and chill until required. Check seasoning, garnish with basil and serve.

Cheese and Herb Creams

Serves 4–6

*If you have any of these left over, they can be shaped into a log, rolled
in cumin seeds or coarsely ground black pepper and served as a cheese
the next day.*

1 oz / 30 g mixed 'soft' herbs, such
  as parsley, chervil, tarragon, dill
  and coriander
5 oz / 140 g plain cottage cheese
5 oz / 140 g plain yoghurt

5 oz / 140 g soft blue cheese
2 garlic cloves, peeled and crushed
fine sea salt
freshly ground white pepper
5 fl oz / 140 ml double cream

Put the herbs in a sieve, and pour boiling water over them to blanch them.
Rinse under cold running water, and then firmly pat dry between layers of kitchen
paper. Chop the herbs finely, and put to one side. Rub the cottage cheese through
a sieve, and mix with the yoghurt and blue cheese until smooth. Stir in the garlic
and herbs, and season lightly with salt and pepper. Whip the double cream, and
fold it into the cheese mixture. Spoon it into a sieve lined with scalded muslin, and
leave to drain for a few hours. Shape into *quenelles* (neat egg shapes) with two
tablespoons, and arrange one or two on individual plates with some salad leaves.

Vegetables with Dips

Vegetables
A mixed selection from:
miniature carrots
blanched baby leeks
baby corn
boiled new potatoes
blanched green beans
blanched mangetout or sugar snap
  peas

blanched or raw cauliflower and
  broccoli florets
celery
chicory
cherry tomatoes
radishes
cooked or raw baby artichokes, thinly
  sliced
fennel bulb, cut into wedges

Serve with one or both of the following dressings, which can be used as dips.

Pinzimonio

Serves 4–6

8 fl oz / 230 ml extra virgin olive oil
sea salt
freshly ground black pepper

Mix thoroughly, adding salt and pepper to taste, and serve in a small bowl to accompany the vegetables.

Herb, Walnut and Lemon Dressing

Serves 4–6

1 tbsp finely chopped chives
1 tbsp finely chopped parsley
1 tsp thyme leaves
2 garlic cloves, peeled and chopped
2 oz / 60 g chopped walnuts

½ tsp sea salt
freshly ground black pepper
2 fl oz / 60 ml walnut oil
¼ pt / 140 ml sunflower or grapeseed oil
juice of ½ lemon

Mix the herbs together in a bowl. Crush the garlic and walnuts with the salt and mix into the herbs. Add pepper to taste, then slowly add the oils and finally the lemon juice.

Artichoke and Asparagus Casserole in Butter and Cider Sauce

Serves 8

12 small or 4 medium globe
  artichokes
2 lb / 900 g green asparagus
3 oz / 85 g unsalted butter
2 oz / 60 g shallots, peeled and
  finely chopped
2 fl oz / 60 ml good dry white wine
¼ pt / 140 ml dry cider

¼ pt / 140 ml vegetable stock or water
6 oz / 170 g diced tomato flesh
8 basil leaves, torn into shreds
3 tbsp crème fraîche *(optional)*
salt
freshly ground black pepper
chervil or parsley

If using medium artichokes, remove all the leaves and the chokes. Put the artichoke bottoms in a bowl of acidulated water. Small artichokes need only the outer leaves and the leaf tips removing. Quarter small artichokes, or slice artichoke bottoms into four or five pieces or cut into wedges. Blanch in boiling water for 5 minutes, then drain. Remove and discard any woody stems from the asparagus, and break into 1½ in / 4 cm pieces. Blanch the asparagus pieces in boiling water for 4–5 minutes, then drain and refresh under cold running water. Reserve the tips for garnish. Melt 1 oz / 30 g butter in a flameproof casserole, and add the shallots, artichoke pieces, white wine and cider. Bring to the boil and cook briskly for a few minutes. Add the stock or water and continue cooking until the artichokes are tender but still firm. Remove the artichokes and boil the cooking liquor until reduced by half. Put the artichokes back in the casserole with the asparagus pieces and bring back to the boil. Add the tomato and basil, stir in the crème fraîche, if using, and season to taste. Warm the asparagus tips by pouring boiling water over them. Divide the vegetables between eight individual dishes, and garnish with asparagus tips and chervil or parsley.

Variations ∾ Courgettes could be used if artichokes are not available, although you would need to adjust the cooking time.

Cook some small new potatoes in the casserole, and serve with some lightly boiled or poached eggs, even quail eggs, to make a marvellous main course.

Vegetable and Tofu Creams with Tomato and Basil Vinaigrette

Serves 6–8

1 onion, peeled and finely chopped
1 tbsp sunflower oil
1 small fennel bulb, trimmed and finely chopped
4 oz / 110 g celeriac *or* 1 celery stalk, trimmed and finely chopped
2 carrots, peeled and finely chopped
2 courgettes, trimmed and finely chopped

1 small aubergine, trimmed and finely chopped
1 small turnip, trimmed and finely chopped
1–2 tbsp chopped parsley
3 eggs
4 oz / 110 g silken tofu (see page 142)
3 fl oz / 85 ml single cream
salt
freshly ground black pepper

Sweat the onion in the oil until soft, then add the rest of the vegetables. Moisten with 2–3 tablespoons water (or dry white wine if you have a bottle opened), cover with a lid, and cook until the vegetables are soft. Add the parsley and put the vegetables in a blender with the eggs, tofu and cream. Blend until smooth, then rub through a sieve and season to taste. Oil or butter six or eight dariole moulds or ramekins, and spoon in the vegetable cream. Steam over a low heat, or cook in a bain-marie in a preheated oven at 170°C / 325°F / Mark 3 until set, when a knife point inserted in the middle will come out clean. Allow the creams to cool a little before turning them out on to plates. Serve with Tomato and Basil Vinaigrette.

Tomato and basil vinaigrette
2–3 ripe tomatoes
4 tbsp extra virgin olive oil
2 tbsp sherry vinegar

sprigs of basil
salt
freshly ground black pepper

Roughly chop the tomatoes, and put in a blender or food processor with the olive oil, vinegar and a few basil leaves. Process and sieve. Season to taste and spoon around the vegetable creams. Garnish with basil leaves, shredded or whole.

Poached and Marinated Vegetables

*Artichoke bottoms and baby artichokes, courgettes, green beans,
celery, mushrooms, wild mushrooms and small onions are some of the
vegetables that can be prepared in this way. Trim the vegetables as
appropriate, cutting celery and courgettes into rounds or batons.
Cooking time will vary: mushrooms and courgettes will need only a
few minutes; onions and artichokes much longer.*

Court bouillon
7 fl oz / 200 ml water or vegetable
  stock
3½ fl oz / 100 ml extra virgin olive
  oil
juice of 2 lemons *or* 3½ fl oz /
  100 ml dry white wine

1 tbsp coriander seeds
1 tsp coarse sea salt
½ tsp white peppercorns
piece of fennel
celery top
sprig of thyme
bay leaf

Put the water or stock, oil, and lemon juice or wine in a large saucepan with the
coriander, salt and peppercorns. Tie the fennel, celery top and herbs together in a
bouquet garni and add it to the pan. Bring to the boil and simmer for 5 minutes,
then add the vegetables and cook them for as long as necessary. Strain them, and
leave both vegetables and cooking liquor to cool. Mix together again when cold,
and serve with crusty French bread or warm rolls.

Fennel with Cheese Sauce

Serves 4

*This is not based on any dish I have ever come across in Italy, but the
inspiration certainly comes from the Italian way with vegetables,
which is to treat them as an important part of any meal.*

4 fennel bulbs, about 8 oz / 230 g
  each
1 oz / 30 g butter
2 shallots, peeled and finely
  chopped

¼ pt / 140 ml full-cream milk
4 oz / 110 g Gorgonzola or Dolcelatte
  cheese
4 oz / 110 g Fontina or Caciotta cheese
4 oz / 110 g ricotta cheese

Trim the feathery tops from the fennel bulbs, and if in good condition, reserve some for garnishing. Remove any bruised or broken leaves. Bring a large saucepan of lightly salted water to the boil. Cut the fennel bulbs in half down the middle, and put them in the boiling water. Bring back to the boil and simmer for 10–20 minutes until just tender. The length of cooking time will depend on how fresh and juicy the fennel was to begin with.

When the fennel is cooked, drain it. Remove the leaves in the centre of each piece, taking great care not to break them. Leave one complete layer of leaves so that a small bowl is formed, in which to pour melted cheese. The leaves you have removed will serve as scoops to eat the cheese with. Some of the broader ones can be cut in half down the middle. Put the separated leaves in a colander, cover and set over hot water to keep them warm.

Melt the butter in a small saucepan and gently fry the shallots until soft. Pour on a little of the milk. Crumble in the blue cheese, cut the Fontina or Caciotta into small cubes, and put these in the pan together with the ricotta. Stir together, heating gently until melted, adding more milk, if required, to give the sauce a homogeneous, creamy consistency. Pour into the fennel 'bowls', and finish under a hot grill so that the cheese *just* begins to brown and bubble. Put on individual plates, garnish with sprigs of fennel tops and serve with the reserved fennel leaves.

Potted Cheese

Serves 4–6

12 oz / 340 g farmhouse cheese, grated or crumbled	2–3 tbsp port or oloroso sherry good pinch of ground mace
4 oz / 110 g unsalted butter, softened	clarified butter

Make sure that the cheese is at room temperature, and mix it with the butter. Add the port or sherry and mace, and mix thoroughly once more. Pack into individual ramekins, and run a spoonful or two of clarified butter over the top to seal it. Refrigerate until required, but allow to come to room temperature before serving with fingers of hot toast. Alternatively, spoon into celery stalks or chicory leaves.

Variation ⁓ Chopped walnuts can be added for further refinement. Potted gorgonzola is excellent. Blend it with an equal quantity of ricotta, and half the quantity of butter. Season with nutmeg and add grappa instead of port or sherry. If using Roquefort, flavour it with Armagnac.

Broccoli with Tomato and Soy Butter

Serves 4

*This dish, with a slightly oriental touch both in its method of cooking
and in its flavours, is good served on its own.*

1 lb / 455 g broccoli	3 tbsp soy sauce
2 tsp sesame oil	1 tbsp rice vinegar or sherry vinegar
1 tbsp salt	3 oz / 85 g chopped tomato flesh
2½ fl oz / 70 ml water or vegetable stock	2 oz / 60 g chilled unsalted butter, diced
	freshly ground white pepper

Separate the broccoli into florets and stalks. Peel the stalks and slice them on
the diagonal to give a large cooking surface. Bring a saucepan of water to the boil
with the sesame oil and salt. Drop in the broccoli, bring it back to the boil and boil
for 30 seconds. Drain quickly and plunge the broccoli into chilled water, or at least
rinse it well under running cold water to cool it quickly.

Heat the water or stock with the soy sauce and vinegar in a wok or large frying
pan. Add the broccoli, cover, and steam until just tender. Remove the broccoli, and
keep it warm over hot water, leaving the cooking juices in the wok or frying pan.
Add the tomato and quickly reduce to 2–3 tablespoons. Off the heat, add the cubes
of butter, one at a time, and whisk into the sauce until it emulsifies and thickens.
Season with a little white pepper. (Extra salt should not be required because of the
salt in the soy sauce.) Serve the sauce and broccoli separately or together, as you
wish.

Carciofi all Romana

(Roman-style Artichokes)

Serves 4

1 lemon
4 globe artichokes
few stems of mint
few stems of parsley

salt
freshly ground black pepper
3 tbsp extra virgin olive oil
4 tbsp white wine

Grate the zest from the lemon, and cut the lemon in half. If the artichokes have long stalks, break these off near the base, and rub the broken surfaces with the cut lemon to keep them from browning. Peel the stalks down to the tender centre, and drop in a bowl of water to which you have added some lemon juice. Break off the coarse outer leaves of the artichokes, and then snip off the coarse tips of the remaining leaves until you have removed all the tough fibrous part. Each cut surface should be rubbed with the lemon to prevent it darkening. The choke is dealt with later. (There is no need to cut off the leaf tips unless you have artichokes with sharp spiny points to the leaves.)

Strip the mint and parsley leaves from the stems. Chop the leaves and put the stems, together with some of the lemon zest, in a large saucepan of water. Season lightly and bring to the boil, then add the artichokes and cook for 15–20 minutes. Drain, and when cool enough to handle, open out the centre and remove the hairy choke without removing the tender base, which is the best part of the artichoke. Put the artichokes back in the pan with the olive oil and white wine, chopped herbs and zest, keeping a little of the green herbs and yellow zest back to sprinkle on the artichokes before serving. Cover and cook over a low heat until the artichokes are tender. Serve in shallow soup plates, scattered with the remaining herbs and zest. Eat with a knife and fork or your fingers.

The peeled stalks can be cooked with the artichokes and then used in soup or as a salad ingredient.

Stilton Mousse

This was devised by Ida van den Hurk, a winner of Holland's Lady Chef competition. It is very easy to make and is best served simply with salad.

6 oz / 170 g Stilton
2½ fl oz / 70 ml single cream
1 tbsp mild clear honey

4 freshly made pancakes (see page 56)
chives *(optional)*

Cream the Stilton with a fork or in a blender or food processor. Blend in the cream and honey. Divide the mixture between the pancakes, and fold into parcels, or tie into bundles with chives. Serve cold, or heat through in the oven for 8–10 minutes.

Light Meals and Snacks

The recipes in this chapter are dishes that can be served equally well for lunch, supper, high tea, or even as a stop-gap between meals. Some, such as Hummus (see page 44), or Aubergine Salad (see page 46), would make good starters, while others, like Roquefort Profiteroles (see page 52) and Cheese Soufflés in Paper Cases (see page 55) could be served with pre-dinner drinks.

You will find here ideas for recipes that can be prepared using little more than the contents of your store-cupboard; many of them are based on eggs or cheese, some to be eaten hot, some cold. A number of the recipes can be prepared in advance and stored in the refrigerator, making them invaluable to the cook faced with unexpected guests, or when an impromptu supper or picnic is suggested.

For food that can be packed into a picnic hamper or lunchbox, choose from the pastry recipes included in the chapter, or try something different, such as Eggs Casho (see page 48), which can be used to fill wholemeal bread rolls. A dish like Radishes with Three Butters (see page 44) makes unusual and varied picnic food. For ease of transportation, pack the butters into lidded plastic containers rather than ramekins.

One of the best ways to enjoy food of this sort is to put several dishes together to make a substantial meal to share with friends. With light savoury dishes like this, it is as easy to cook for a crowd as for a couple. The ingredients are not expensive, especially if you have a prolific vegetable garden or allotment, of if you have access to a good farm shop or street market. The food does not take very long to cook and is not complicated. Six or eight dishes, a platter of boiled or baked rice, perhaps a salad and some bread, and you have an unusual meal that everyone will enjoy.

Stir-fried Vegetables and Toasted Sesame Tartlets

Makes 24

24 thin slices bread

2–3 tbsp groundnut (peanut) oil, plus extra for frying

1 tbsp toasted sesame oil

2 tbsp sesame seeds

1 in / 2.5 cm piece of fresh root ginger, peeled and sliced

2–3 star anise

2 in / 5 cm cinnamon stick

1 lb / 455 g prepared vegetables, selected from thin slices of carrot, mushrooms, baby corn cobs, broccoli florets, mangetout and spring onions

1 tbsp soy sauce

1 tbsp amontillado sherry or rice wine

1 tbsp sherry vinegar or rice vinegar

pinch of freshly ground black pepper or crushed Szechuan peppercorns

Cut the bread slices into 24 rounds with a pastry cutter. Brush 24 bun tins with some of the groundnut oil, and mix the rest with half the sesame oil. Use this to brush the bread, and press each piece into a bun tin. Sprinkle a few sesame seeds into each. Lightly toast the rest of the sesame seeds in a small frying pan and set aside. Bake the tartlets in a preheated oven at 200°C / 400°F / Mark 6 for 10–15 minutes, until crisp and golden.

Meanwhile, put 2–3 tablespoons groundnut oil in a frying pan or wok, and gently fry the ginger, star anise and cinnamon for 5 minutes. Remove from the oil, and then add the vegetables to the pan, starting with those that take longest to cook, and finishing with the mushrooms and spring onions. Stir continuously as the vegetables are frying, and when all have been added, splash in the soy sauce, sherry or wine, vinegar and pepper, together with 1–2 tablespoons of cold water. Cover with the lid and steam for a few minutes, shaking occasionally. When the vegetables are just cooked, but still crisp and vivid, stir in the remaining sesame oil, and spoon them into the hot tartlet cases. Sprinkle with toasted sesame seeds before serving.

Gougère

Serves 6–8

*Using the standard choux pastry recipe (see below), you can make a
versatile cheese dish to be served as a light supper dish with salad.
Gruyère is the cheese used in the authentic version, but you could
substitute other hard cheeses. Individual gougères made with Gruyère
are traditionally served in the cellars of Burgundy and Chablis when
wine-tasting.*

3 oz / 85 g Gruyère cheese, finely diced
12 oz / 340 g choux pastry

Mix the diced cheese with the pastry and spoon it into a ring on a greased
baking sheet. To make it rise even more by creating a steam oven, invert a deep
roasting tin or cake tin over the pastry. Bake the pastry in a preheated oven at
220°C / 425°F / Mark 7 for 15 minutes, then turn the heat down to 180°C /
350°F / Mark 4 for another 12–15 minutes. Remove and serve hot or warm.

Variation ⸻ Mix diced mature goat's cheese with the pastry before baking
and, when cool, split the gougère horizontally and sandwich it back together with a
filling of fresh goat's cheese mixed with yoghurt or cream and fresh herbs.

Choux Pastry

½ pt / 280 ml water
4 oz / 110 g butter
½ tsp salt

5 oz / 140 g plain flour, sifted
4 eggs, lightly beaten

Put the water, butter and salt in a saucepan and bring to the boil. When it does
so, tip in all the flour at once, stirring vigorously with a wooden spoon. As you stir,
the mixture will dry and become smooth to the point where it leaves the sides of
the pan. Remove from the heat, and beat in the eggs, a little at a time, making sure
each addition is thoroughly incorporated. Keep stirring until you have a smooth
paste.

Spanakopitta

*This dish, based on a Greek recipe, is very good hot, cold or warm. It
is also as at home in a picnic basket as on the dining-table. I like to
use a mixture of cheeses – feta for sharpness, ricotta or cottage cheese
for mellowness and a hard cheese, which melts and holds the filling
together.*

2¼ lb / 1 kg spinach
6 oz / 170 g butter
salt
freshly ground black pepper
freshly grated nutmeg

3 oz / 85 g ricotta or cottage cheese
2 oz / 60 g feta cheese, crumbled
2 oz / 60 g Parmesan, Pecorino,
    Cheddar or Gruyère cheese, grated
10 sheets filo pastry

Wash and pick over the spinach, and remove any tough central stalks. Shake
dry, and put in a large saucepan with a third of the butter. Cover and cook until
the spinach has wilted and collapsed. Drain and cool the spinach, and season with
salt, pepper and nutmeg. Stir in the cheeses.

Thickly butter a square or round cake tin, about 1–1½ in / 2.5–4 cm deep and 8
in / 20.5 cm across. Melt the remaining butter and brush each sheet of filo pastry
with it before peeling the sheet off the pile. Line the tin with five sheets of buttered
filo, butter side down, and spoon in the spinach mixture. Cut the remaining five
sheets of pastry to fit the top of the pie. Lay two sheets on top, and then bring the
overlapping lining sheets over the top layer of pastry. To finish the pie, lay the last
three sheets of pastry on top. Bake in a preheated oven at 180°C / 350°F / Mark 4
for about 45 minutes, increasing the heat for the last 10 minutes or so to brown the
top. Remove from the oven and allow to cool slightly. Remove from the tin by
inverting a plate over the pie, turning it out, and then putting another plate over
the base of the pie and turning it the right way up.

Llapingachos
(Potato and Cheese Cakes)

Makes 16–20

These come from Ecuador. We ate them frequently in La Choza, a lovely restaurant in Quito. Serve these small ones as hot appetizers to accompany drinks.

2 lb / 900 g floury potatoes	1 onion, peeled and finely chopped
salt	2 tbsp olive oil
freshly ground black pepper	4 oz / 110 g hard cheese, such as
2 oz / 60 g butter	Jarlsberg, Gruyère or Cheddar, grated

Peel, boil and mash the potatoes with salt, pepper and half the butter. Fry the onion in half the olive oil until soft and golden. Allow to cool slightly, and then mix with the cheese. Form the potato into small patties, and bury some of the cheese and onion mixture in the centre. Heat the remaining butter and olive oil in a frying pan, and fry the potato cakes on both sides until golden brown.

Variation ∾ A meal-size version uses the same ingredients to make 6 cakes, which are fried as described and served with a fried egg on top of each. Sliced avocados and a peanut sauce are the other accompaniments.

Potato Pancakes

Makes 18–20

2 oz / 60 g potato flour	1 egg, lightly beaten
2 oz / 60 g plain flour	½ pt / 280 ml water or milk
pinch of salt	3 oz / 85 g grated potato *(optional)*

Sift the flours and salt together, add the egg, and gradually beat in the liquid until smooth. Stir in the potato, if using. Heat a griddle or large heavy frying pan and grease it. Spoon on the batter, 1 tablespoon at a time. The pan may be large enough to cook three or four pancakes at once. Cook until the tops of the pancakes are set, then turn and cook the other side. Remove the pancakes from the pan, grease the pan again, and continue until all the batter is used.

Cheese and Asparagus Pastries

Makes 8

*Buying asparagus loose during the short season, one is often left with
an assortment of different sizes. Here is one way of using them up.*

8 oz / 230 g trimmed fresh
asparagus (the tender green parts
and tips only)
1 lb / 455 g puff pastry
8 oz / 230 g cheese, grated
4 ripe tomatoes, peeled, deseeded
and chopped

salt
freshly ground black pepper
juice of ½ lemon
8 basil leaves
2 oz / 60 g butter
milk or beaten egg, to glaze

Bring a saucepan of salted water to the boil and throw in the asparagus. Boil
vigorously for 5 minutes, or until just beginning to become tender. Drain and
refresh under cold running water. Roll out the puff pastry, and cut out eight circles.
Divide the asparagus between the eight circles, arranging it on one half only.
Divide the cheese into eight and heap it up on top of the asparagus. Top this with
the chopped tomatoes. Season to taste with salt, pepper and a little lemon juice.

Tear the basil leaves into shreds, and arrange on top of the tomato, together
with a small knob of butter. Moisten around the edges of the pastry circles with
water, fold them over and seal the parcels. Place on a greased baking sheet and
brush with milk or egg. Pierce the top of each pastry with a fork to let the steam
escape, and bake for 15 minutes in a preheated oven at 190°C / 375°F / Mark 5.

Grilled Polenta Slices with Mushrooms

Makes 16–20 slices

This recipe is based on one from Antonio Carluccio's excellent book,
An Invitation to Italian Cooking. *If fresh ceps are hard to find,*
ordinary field mushrooms combined with a few dried ceps still give a
wonderful flavour to this dish. It is best to start your preparation the
day before, to allow sufficient time for the polenta to set.

Polenta Slices
3 pt / 1.70 l water
salt
13 oz / 370 g packet polenta *or*
   10 oz / 280 g yellow polenta flour

1 oz / 30 g butter
2 oz / 60 g Parmesan cheese, freshly
   grated
2 tbsp olive oil

Put the water in a large saucepan, add salt and bring to the boil. Very carefully add the polenta, stirring constantly to prevent lumps forming. Continue to stir until you see the golden mass start to come away from the sides of the pan (5 minutes for polenta; 30 minutes for ordinary polenta flour). Stir in the butter and the Parmesan cheese, and, while it is still hot, pour into an oiled mould with straight sides, such as a loaf tin. Leave to cool and set, ideally overnight.

Next day, turn out the polenta, and cut it into slices about ¾ in / 2 cm thick. Brush each slice with olive oil, and put under a hot grill until well browned on both sides. Serve with a small spoonful of the mushroom sauce (see below) on top of each slice.

Mushroom Sauce
12 oz / 340 g fresh ceps *or* 12 oz /
   340 g field mushrooms plus
   1 oz / 30 g dried ceps
1 small onion, peeled and finely
   chopped
3 tbsp olive oil

1 oz / 30 g butter
7 oz / 200 g can peeled plum tomatoes,
   puréed
salt
freshly ground black pepper
6 basil leaves, chopped (*optional*)

Clean and slice the mushrooms, and, if using dried ceps, soak them in lukewarm water for 10 minutes. Fry the onion in the olive oil and butter until translucent, then add the mushrooms, and cook over a high heat for 10 minutes. Add the tomatoes, lower the heat slightly, and continue cooking for another 20 minutes, so that most of the water from the tomatoes evaporates. Season to taste with salt and pepper, and, if using, stir in the basil.

Variations ∾ Grilled polenta slices make a good 'bed' for all manner of savouries. Try them with aubergine purée, olive paste, or any of the toppings, spreads, pâtés, sauces and fillings found in this chapter and throughout the book.

See also Creamy Cep Polenta on page 129.

Roasted Garlic, Gorgonzola and Toasted Pinenuts

Per person

I have tasted various versions of this dish in California and I am fairly sure that Alice Waters, of Chez Panisse in Berkeley, is the originator.

1 large head of garlic
1 tbsp extra virgin olive oil
2–3 oz / 60–85 g slice of
   Gorgonzola cheese

1 tbsp pinenuts
greenery, to garnish

Peel off any loose skin, but leave the garlic bulb whole. With a sharp knife, slice off a shallow cap from the top of the bulb. Put the garlic in a baking tin and sprinkle the cut surface with the olive oil, letting the rest dribble into the tin. Replace the cap, and bake in the centre of a preheated oven at 190°C / 375°F / Mark 5 for 20 minutes. Lower the heat to 150°C / 300°F / Mark 2, and continue cooking until the garlic is creamy and tender, which may take 1 hour altogether. Meanwhile, put the cheese on a heatproof plate and toast the pinenuts in a dry frying pan.

Just before you are ready to serve the garlic, melt the cheese in the oven or under the grill. Put the garlic on the plate, cap removed, and scatter the pinenuts on the cheese. Garnish the plate with greenery.

Radishes with Three Butters

Serves 4–6

I imagine eating this lovely summery snack in a shaded garden or taking it on a picnic.

3–4 bunches of radishes, trimmed
8 oz / 230 g salted butter, at room temperature
1 ripe tomato, peeled, deseeded and chopped

few sprigs of watercress, blanched and finely chopped
2 oz / 60 g mushrooms, fried and chopped
freshly ground black pepper

Pile the radishes into a serving bowl. Divide the butter into three, and into each portion, mix one of the next three ingredients. Season with pepper, and pack each butter into a small ramekin. Serve with crusty bread and a bowl of coarse salt.

Instead of using butter, you can serve yoghurt dips flavoured with the ingredients above, adding appropriate herbs; for example, basil with the tomato, and chives with the mushrooms. Ripe avocados and cucumber can also be used to make flavoured butters or yoghurts.

Hummus

Serves 4

The sesame oil used in this recipe is not the toasted light brown sesame oil of Chinese cooking, but clear virgin sesame oil. The sesame paste is available at good delicatessens and Cypriot shops.

1 lb / 455 g cooked or canned chick peas, drained
2 garlic cloves, peeled and crushed
juice of ½ lemon
2½ fl oz / 70 ml extra virgin olive oil

1 tbsp sesame oil or sesame paste (tahina)
salt
freshly ground black pepper
coriander leaves, to garnish

Put the chick peas in a blender or food processor with the rest of the ingredients. Process until smooth, then spoon into a bowl and trickle a little more olive oil on top. Garnish with coriander, and serve with olives, hot pitta bread, sesame bread sticks and raw vegetables.

Pizzas

Makes 2

*These are best made when you are making bread. The bases can be
frozen until required. Smaller versions can be made as canapés.*

6–8 oz / 170–230 g white bread
   dough (see page 152)
2 tbsp extra virgin olive oil
coarse sea salt
freshly ground black pepper

3–4 oz / 85–110 g goat's cheese, sliced
4 tomatoes, peeled, deseeded and
   chopped
12 black olives, pitted and chopped
basil leaves, shredded

Cut the dough in half and roll out two circles. Place them on an oiled baking
sheet, brush them with olive oil, and sprinkle with salt and pepper. Allow to rise
for 20–30 minutes, and bake in the top half of a preheated oven at 200°C / 400°F /
Mark 6 for about 10 minutes, until crisp and puffy. Remove from the oven, and
allow to cool slightly before covering with cheese and topping with chopped
tomatoes and olives. Scatter shredded basil leaves over the pizzas to finish.

Poached Eggs in Field Mushrooms

Serves 4

4 large hollow field mushrooms
3 oz / 85 g butter, melted
4 eggs
2–3 tbsp grated cheese

salt
freshly ground black pepper
paprika

Brush or peel the mushrooms, as necessary. Remove the stalks, trim off the
ends and chop finely. Brush the mushroom caps all over with melted butter. Place
the chopped trimmings in the centre of the caps together with any remaining
butter, and grill or bake the mushrooms until tender. Meanwhile, poach the eggs,
and drain them on kitchen paper. Place a poached egg on each cooked mushroom,
sprinkle with grated cheese, salt, pepper and paprika to taste, and finish off under
the grill until the cheese melts.

   Variations ∾ Add a spoonful of pesto, a smear of mustard or a splash of
cream to the mushrooms before the eggs, or, if you can get quail eggs, you can try
miniature versions of this dish, using cap or button mushrooms.

Aubergine Salad

Serves 4

1 aubergine, about 1 lb / 455 g
garlic cloves, to taste
3 heaped tbsp finely chopped
   parsley
pinch of fresh or dried thyme or
   oregano

extra virgin olive oil
salt
freshly ground black pepper

Slice the aubergine in half lengthways. Preheat the grill until very hot, and put the aubergine under it, skin-side up. Grill for 15 minutes, until the skin is wrinkled and charred, but not burnt. This is, of course, difficult to see, but your sense of touch and smell will tell you when it is charred. Remove from the grill, and when cool enough to handle, scoop out the softened flesh with a pointed teaspoon. Put this in a sieve over a bowl so that some of the liquid drains away. The flesh tends to come away in long strands, so snip these up with kitchen scissors. Transfer the aubergine to a bowl. Peel and crush the garlic cloves, and stir into the aubergine. Add the herbs, olive oil and season to taste. Serve as it is, with hot toast or warm pitta bread, or on a plate of salad leaves garnished with olives and tomatoes.

Frittata of Wild Greens

Serves 4

8 oz / 230 g wild greens, washed,
   blanched, dried and chopped (see
   page 98)
2 tbsp olive oil

1 oz / 30 g butter
6 eggs
freshly ground black pepper
salt

Gently fry the greens for a few minutes in the oil and butter in an omelette pan. Lightly beat the eggs, with a little pepper and salt, and pour over the greens. When the underside is set, turn the frittata over and cook briefly on the other side before sliding it on to a warm serving plate.

Variations ⁓ Cheese can also be added to the beaten egg – grated Parmesan, crumbled blue cheese or diced mozzarella.

Diced potatoes fried in the pan before the greens will turn this into a more substantial dish similar to a Spanish omelette (see page 135).

Asparagus and Potato Omelette

Serves 4

8 oz / 230 g cooked potatoes, diced
2 tbsp olive oil
6–8 oz / 170–230 g cooked
  asparagus, diced

9 eggs, beaten
salt
freshly ground black pepper

Fry the potatoes in the olive oil until just golden brown. Heat an omelette pan, and smear with a little more olive oil. Stir the asparagus and potatoes into the eggs with a little seasoning. Pour the mixture into the pan, shaking it and turning the eggs with a spatula to encourage them to set. Turn the heat down, and let the mixture begin to cook through. Once it is fairly firm, invert a plate over the pan and turn the pan over so that the omelette comes out flat on to the plate. Slide the omelette back into the pan to cook the second side. Turn the cooked omelette out on to a plate and leave to cool slightly before cutting into wedges and serving warm.

Variation ∾ Make individual omelettes, using 2–3 eggs for each, and fill with a few cooked asparagus stalks and diced potatoes fried as above.

Pipérade

Serves 2–3

2 red peppers
1 green pepper
1 onion, peeled and finely chopped
2 tbsp olive oil *or* 1 oz / 30 g butter
8 oz / 230 g ripe tomatoes, peeled,
  deseeded and chopped

6 eggs
salt
freshly ground black pepper
cayenne pepper or chilli powder, to
  taste

Char and skin the peppers, then deseed and chop them. Cook with the onion in the olive oil or butter until soft. Add the tomatoes, and continue cooking until you have a thick purée. Lightly beat the eggs. Lower the heat under the pan, and once the mixture is no longer boiling, stir in the eggs. Season with salt and pepper, and cayenne or chilli powder, and continue stirring over a low heat until the eggs are cooked to a cream. They should not be lumpy but should have amalgamated with the purée and thickened it. Serve immediately with toast or fried bread.

Eggs Casho

Serves 6–8

1–2 tbsp sunflower or walnut oil
1 celery stalk, trimmed and thinly
  sliced
1 carrot, peeled and shredded
1 leek *or* 6 spring onions, trimmed
  and thinly sliced diagonally
4 oz / 110 g oyster, shiitake or
  button mushrooms, cleaned and
  sliced or quartered

4 oz / 110 g bean sprouts, blanched and
  drained
8–10 eggs
2–3 tbsp soy sauce

Heat the oil in a wok or large frying pan, and toss in the celery and carrot. Stir-fry for 2–3 minutes, then add the leek or onions and the mushrooms. Stir-fry for a further 2–3 minutes, then add the bean sprouts. Beat the eggs with the soy sauce, and pour over the vegetables. Turn with a spatula until just beginning to set. Serve immediately.

Variation ∞ Cold, this makes a delicious filling for slightly hollowed out wholemeal bread rolls.

Mild Curried Potato Omelette

Serves 4–6

This omelette is best served freshly cooked and warm.

2 tbsp groundnut (peanut) or
  sunflower oil
1 lb / 455 g new potatoes, scrubbed
  and sliced or cubed
½ tsp ground turmeric
1 tsp ground cumin
1 tsp ground coriander
seeds of 6–8 cardamom pods,
  crushed

½ tsp mustard seed, crushed
2½ fl oz / 70 ml coconut milk or water
1–2 tbsp chopped watercress or rocket
  (optional)
6–8 eggs, beaten
salt
freshly ground black pepper
cayenne pepper

Heat half the oil in a heavy saucepan, add the potatoes, turn them in the oil for a few minutes, and then add the spices. Cook together for a few minutes more until the potatoes are coated with the spices. Add the liquid, bring to the boil, reduce the heat as low as possible, partially cover the pan, and cook until the potatoes are tender, by which time the liquid should just about have been absorbed or evaporated. (If the potatoes show signs of drying out before they are cooked, add more liquid.) Remove from the heat.

Heat an omelette pan, and add the rest of the oil. Stir the potatoes and greens, if using, into the eggs and season with salt, pepper and cayenne. Tip the whole lot into the omelette pan and cook until the underside is firm and brown and the top beginning to set. Slide the omelette out on to a plate, still flat, and then turn it upside-down in the pan to cook the second side. Turn out and allow to cool slightly before cutting into wedges and serving with salad.

Pisto Manchego

Serves 6

The best time to make this dish, which originates in La Mancha, is at the end of summer, when tomatoes are sweet and ripe.

2 mild onions, peeled and chopped
about 6 tbsp extra virgin olive oil
1 green pepper, deseeded and cut into strips or chunks
1 red pepper, deseeded and cut into strips or chunks
1 lb / 455 g firm, ripe, sweet tomatoes, deseeded and chopped
1 lb / 455 g courgettes, trimmed and diced or sliced
3 or 4 garlic cloves, peeled and crushed
¼ pt / 140 ml water
salt
freshly ground black pepper
6 eggs
finely chopped fresh parsley

Fry the onions in 6 tablespoons olive oil until transparent. Add all the other vegetables and the garlic to the onions, with a little more olive oil, if necessary, and the water. Cook until you have a rich vegetable stew. Season to taste, then divide the vegetables between six oiled individual ovenproof dishes. Make a well in the centre of each, slide in an egg, and bake in a preheated oven at 190°C / 375°F / Mark 5 for 5–10 minutes or until the eggs are done the way you like them. Scatter on parsley and serve.

Fonduta

Serves 4

*This Italian recipe is lighter than fondue (see page 132), and is good
served on toast or poured over grilled polenta slices (see page 42). You
could also try it with steamed new potatoes and a mixture of baby
vegetables as a starter.*

3 eggs
½ pt / 280 ml full-cream milk
2 oz / 60 g unsalted butter
5 oz / 140 g hard cheese (see
    suggestions for Cheese Fondue on
    page 132), grated

salt
freshly ground black pepper
freshly grated nutmeg

Beat the eggs with half of the milk and put in an enamel saucepan with the
butter, cheese and remaining milk. Set over a low heat and stir continuously until
the cheese has melted and a thick cream is produced. Season to taste with salt,
pepper and nutmeg.

Grilled Goat's Cheese on Country Bread

Serves 8

8 slices rustic bread
1 large garlic clove, peeled
extra virgin olive oil

8 slices goat's cheese *or* 8 whole Crottin
    de Chavignol cheeses, or similar

Put the bread under the grill, and toast one side only. Rub the untoasted side
quickly with garlic, brush with olive oil, and put a piece of cheese on each piece of
bread. Put back under the grill and toast until the cheese is browned and bubbling.
The heat will be sufficient to soften the cheese to a spreading consistency. Serve
immediately.

Variations ∾ After rubbing the untoasted side of the bread with garlic, place a
few leaves of radicchio on each piece, sprinkle liberally with olive oil, season, and
place under the grill until the radicchio has browned slightly. Lay the cheese on top
of each slice, and return to the grill for a few minutes until the cheese is lightly
browned and bubbling.

Gruyère and Courgette Batter Pudding

Serves 4–6

*Traditionally a sweet dish made with cherries, the recipe adapts well
to savoury ingredients.*

3 tbsp strong plain white flour
¾ pt / 430 ml full-cream milk
3 eggs
2 oz / 60 g butter
6 oz / 170 g Gruyère cheese, diced

4 oz / 110 g courgettes, trimmed and
   sliced
salt
freshly ground black pepper

Beat the flour, milk and eggs together to make a smooth batter, and let it stand
for 30 minutes. Use half the butter to grease a flan dish. Scatter the diced Gruyère
and the courgette slices over the base of the dish. Season the batter with salt and
pepper, and pour it into the dish. Dot the rest of the butter on top. Bake in a
preheated oven at 200°C / 400°F / Mark 6 for 30 minutes, and then at 180°C /
350°F / Mark 4 for another 20 minutes. Remove from the oven; the mixture will
have risen and become puffy when first taken from the oven, but will then sink. Do
not worry; it is meant to do this. Serve warm.

Variations ～ Other vegetables and cheeses can be experimented with.

Courgettes and cheese are also good when baked in a custard rather than a
batter mixture. Beat together 3 eggs and ½ pt / 280 ml milk, season, and pour this
over the courgette slices and cheese in the flan dish. Bake for 30 minutes at 180°C /
350°F / Mark 4, and serve warm.

Traditional Baked Rarebit

Serves 4

1 oz / 30 g butter
8 oz / 230 g farmhouse Lancashire
  cheese, crumbled
2½ fl oz / 70 ml real ale

pinch of English mustard powder
dash of vegetarian Worcestershire sauce
freshly ground white pepper
4 slices bread, toasted on one side

Melt the butter in a saucepan, and stir in the cheese, ale, mustard powder, Worcestershire sauce and pepper. Stir until the cheese has melted and the mixture is creamy. Put each slice of toast in a small heated ovenproof dish, toasted side down, and pour the mixture over the top. Put briefly in a hot oven, or under the grill, to brown lightly. Serve immediately.

Variations ∾ Some variations add a poached egg on top of the browned cheese. I am not sure that this is an improvement. However, because tomato goes so well with cheese, I might serve a grilled half tomato or a spoonful of tomato chutney with the rarebit. Lancashire is not the only cheese for a rarebit, but I think it is the best; you may prefer Cheshire, Caerphilly or Wensleydale, or an alternative vegetarian cheese.

Roquefort Profiteroles

Makes 18

¼ pt / 140 ml milk and water mixed
2 oz / 60 g butter
3 oz / 85 g plain flour, sifted
pinch of salt

2 large eggs
2 oz / 60 g Roquefort cheese, finely
  diced

Put the liquid and butter in a saucepan, heat gently until the butter has melted, and then bring to a strong boil. Remove from the heat, and tip in the flour and salt. Beat vigorously until the mixture becomes a stiff paste and leaves the sides of the pan. Cool for 5–10 minutes, and then beat in the eggs, one at a time, stirring in vigorously until the dough becomes smooth and glossy. Stir in the cheese. Drop teaspoonfuls of the mixture on to a greased baking sheet, and bake for 10–12 minutes in the top half of a preheated oven at 200°C / 400°F / Mark 6. Switch off the heat, open the oven door slightly, and leave the profiteroles in the oven for another 3–5 minutes. Remove and serve while hot.

SOUFFLÉS

WHENEVER I make a soufflé, I am always so pleased with the result that I promise myself to make them more often. But I never remember to do so. Yet we all, almost certainly, have all the ingredients necessary in our store-cupboards or refrigerators: eggs, milk, flour, butter and a little something to add in the way of texture and flavour are all it takes to create a fine impressive dish.

Soufflés are easy to make and make ideal light meals, served with a salad or vegetables. Peter Kromberg, of the InterContinental Hotel in London, is the acknowledged expert, and a few years ago, I spent several weeks in his kitchen, where I picked up a number of tips on how to create the perfect soufflé:

- Use egg whites that are 4–5 days old for the best results, and always make sure the whisk you beat them with is scrupulously clean and grease-free.
- Fold the whisked egg whites into the basic mixture while it is still warm, as this helps the soufflé to rise.
- When filling the soufflé dish, do it carefully so that no drips hit the edge of the soufflé dish. This interferes with the rising action, 'anchoring' the soufflé to the dish.
- A soufflé dish can be prepared in different ways according to the type of soufflé. It should be well buttered, and then dusted with grated Parmesan, with breadcrumbs, pin-head oatmeal or sugar, depending on whether you are making a savoury or a sweet soufflé. This preparation also makes it easier to remove small soufflés from ramekins if you want to serve them sitting in a pool of sauce.
- The correct consistency of a soufflé should be soft enough in the centre so that each serving from a large soufflé will have some of the firmer outer portion, together with a little of the soft centre, which will be almost like a sauce.

Basic Savoury Soufflé

Serves 6–8

1 pt / 570 ml milk	2 oz / 60 g butter
salt	8 eggs, 6 of them separated
freshly ground black pepper	2½ oz / 70 g plain flour, sifted
freshly grated nutmeg	3 oz / 85 g cheese, grated

Butter a soufflé dish or dishes, and dust with a little grated Parmesan. Put three-quarters of the milk in a saucepan with the seasoning and butter. Bring to the boil. Beat the two whole eggs with the six egg yolks, the flour and the remaining milk, and stir slowly into the boiling milk over a low heat. Stir continuously until the mixture thickens but does not curdle. Remove from the heat. Whisk the egg whites until stiff. Stir the cheese into the sauce, and then fold in the egg white. Pour into the prepared dish or dishes, and bake in a preheated oven at 200°C / 400°F / Mark 6 for 12–22 minutes, depending on the size of the dish(es).

Savoury Soufflé Variations

Some of Peter Kromberg's specialities include an artichoke soufflé baked in its shell with a warm mustard vinaigrette; an aubergine soufflé with a red pepper and mint sauce; and a celery, pear and walnut soufflé with a port and Stilton sauce, which sounds a very agreeable combination. Strongly flavoured cheeses produce very good soufflés, I find. Michel Bourdin of the Connaught Hotel in London serves individual Stilton soufflés baked in pastry cases. Alice Waters at Chez Panisse in Berkeley, California, devised a recipe for a shallow soufflé with goat's cheese. This is a delightfully homely dish when baked in rustic earthenware. It cooks more quickly because the mixture is not as deep as the classic soufflé.

I feel much the same way about soufflés as I do about omelettes when it comes to deciding what to put in them. Although it sounds unlikely, potatoes are just as good in a soufflé as they are in an omelette; diced, cooked firm waxy salad potatoes, and some well-flavoured fairly hard goat's cheese, such as Mendip, added to the basic savoury soufflé mix before folding in the egg whites. Serve the soufflé with a fresh tomato sauce.

Cheese Soufflés in Paper Cases

Makes 12

*These light miniature soufflés are ideal for serving as a savoury snack
with drinks.*

2 tbsp melted butter or sunflower oil	7 fl oz / 200 ml milk, boiled
1 oz / 30 g butter	3 oz / 85 g hard cheese, grated
1 oz / 30 g plain flour	1 egg yolk
	2 egg whites

Brush 12 fluted paper bun cases with the melted butter or oil, and place on a baking sheet. Make a thick, smooth white sauce with the butter, flour and milk, and cook for 5–10 minutes. Remove from the heat, add the cheese, and stir until melted. Beat in the egg yolk. Whisk the whites until firm, and fold into the egg and cheese mixture. Spoon into paper cases to within ½ in / 1 cm of the top, and run a knife tip or teaspoon around the top edge of the mixture to help it rise. Bake in a preheated oven at 180°C / 350°F / Mark 4 for 10–15 minutes.

Sauces with Soufflés

Opening the top of a soufflé at the table and pouring in a hot sauce has a spectacular effect, causing it to puff up in its dish, to *souffler* in fact. With a spoon in each hand, gently prize apart the top crust, and immediately pour in the sauce.

The same uncooked sauces that go well with pasta can also be used with savoury soufflés. Try fresh tomato and basil sauce, nothing but the shredded herb mixed with peeled, seeded and diced tomatoes and a little seasoning, with a cheese soufflé. Or pour pesto thinned down with a little olive oil or vegetable stock into a Parmesan soufflé.

PANCAKES

PANCAKES are extremely versatile. They can be served with a huge variety of toppings and fillings, both sweet and savoury. When we were children, my mother would make pancakes for my brother and me on Shrove Tuesday. We would smear them with butter, then sprinkle them with lemon juice and sugar, and roll up and eat them as fast as she could make them.

Cheese, artichoke hearts, asparagus, spinach, mushrooms, onions and tomatoes all make good fillings for savoury pancakes, either alone or combined. Let your imagination flow freely.

Whilst making pancake batter is relatively easy, achieving a thin pancake that doesn't stick first time is not. I usually plan for at least the first two to go into the waste bin. I find a well-seasoned, cast-iron crêpe pan is best for the job. I bought one in France which I only use for pancakes. I never wash it, only oil it.

Pancakes
(Basic Recipe)

Makes 6–8

4 oz / 110 g plain or self-raising
   flour
pinch of salt
1 large egg

½ pt / 280 ml milk
grapeseed or other neutral oil for
   cooking

Sift the flour and salt together into a bowl. Stir in the egg, and gradually add the milk, beating until a smooth batter is formed, then whisk to lighten it. Cover the batter and allow to stand for at least 1 hour before using.

Heat a crêpe pan or heavy, flat-bottomed frying pan and brush the inside surface with a little grapeseed or other neutral oil. Pour on just enough batter to coat the base of the pan thinly. Cook until the underside is lightly browned and the top is bubbling. Flip the pancake over, and cook on the other side for 15–20 seconds only. Brush the pan lightly again with oil before cooking the next pancake.

As they come out of the pan, stack the pancakes on a plate over a pan of hot water and cover with a clean, folded tea-towel until required. Spread with the filling of your choice, roll or fold up, and serve.

Another way of serving pancakes is in the style of an old-fashioned quire, where thin pancakes sandwiched with filling are piled one on top of the other, and then cut into wedges like a cake.

Variation ∽ For walnut pancakes, use an extra egg to make the basic batter, and then stir in 2 teaspoons walnut oil and 3 oz / 85 g finely chopped walnuts. Leave this batter to stand for at least 1 hour, then cook the pancakes as above. These are good served with honey or maple syrup, or a syrup made by heating together clear honey, walnut oil and orange juice with a little grated nutmeg.

Buckwheat Galettes

Makes 6–8

4 oz / 110 g buckwheat flour
pinch of salt
1 large egg

1 tbsp grapeseed oil
½ pt / 280 ml warm water

Put the flour in a bowl. Make a well in the centre, and put in the salt, egg and oil. Gradually stir in the warm water until you have a smooth paste. Beat vigorously for a few minutes, and then allow the batter to stand for 1 hour. This resting time, together with the beating and the temperature of the water, helps the flour to swell, which produces the correct texture for the batter.

Cook the pancakes as in the previous recipe, and serve with the filling of your choice. Buckwheat galettes are usually served with a savoury filling; these are sturdy, substantial wodges, not lacy delicate crêpes.

Salads and Side Dishes

The dishes which follow are designed to be more than just accompaniments; each will add interest and variety to a meal by introducing unusual combinations of flavours, as in, for example, Fennel and Pomegranate Salad (see page 61) and Pea and Herb Salad with Raspberry Dressing (see page 64).

The most important thing to remember when making salads is to use good quality, fresh ingredients. The second most important aspect is the dressing. A simple vinaigrette of oil, vinegar and a little seasoning is hard to beat. Nut oils, herbs, garlic and spices are all optional additions. However, the few ingredients needed for a good vinaigrette are worth choosing with care. Look for the best oils and vinegars, and those that you know you like. Extra virgin olive oil is the best oil to use for a vinaigrette. A good vinegar to choose is a traditionally made wine vinegar from France, or balsamic vinegar from Modena in Italy, or perhaps a good sherry vinegar. Only a little sherry vinegar is needed to give an exquisite nutty flavour. It is a particularly good match for tomatoes or a green salad when mixed with a fruity extra virgin olive oil.

Almost all the side dishes in this chapter can be served hot, and are to serve as accompaniments to hot main course food. As well as some interesting vegetable combinations, you will find recipes for plainer accompaniments, such as Basmati Rice (see page 85), and Bulgar Wheat (see page 86). Both are ideal for serving with vegetable stews, casseroles and curries, as is couscous. Made from semolina grains that have been dampened, rolled into small balls or 'grains', and coated with a fine wheat flour, couscous is, properly speaking, a pasta, but it is treated as a grain. Because it is processed, it simply needs moistening or steaming before serving to make it swell and become tender. Simply place the couscous in a colander or sieve over a saucepan of boiling water, cover and allow to heat up and moisten in the steam for 20–30 minutes. About 8 oz / 230 g couscous will be sufficient for four to six people. Couscous also makes an excellent salad (see page 68). (See also Vegetable Couscous, page 104.) Millet and quinoa can also be prepared in this way. Quinoa is a tiny, round grain, about the size of a sesame seed, and, like millet, when cooked fluffs up to yield about four times its original volume.

Whole grains and seeds, such as buckwheat groats and wheat berries, can also be cooked and eaten as hot side dishes. Because, like brown rice, the hard outer coating has not been removed, they take longer to cook but have more nutritional value. The more unusual grains and seeds are generally available from health food shops.

Marinated Carrot Salad

Serves 4–6

1 lb / 455 g carrots, peeled and very
    thinly sliced
4 tbsp extra virgin olive oil
1 tbsp lemon juice, wine vinegar or
    fruit vinegar
1 tsp chopped herbs

3 garlic cloves, peeled and crushed
salt
freshly ground black pepper
2 mild sweet onions, peeled and thinly
    sliced

Drop the carrots into boiling water and cook for 1–2 minutes. Meanwhile, mix
the oil, lemon juice or vinegar, herbs, garlic and seasoning. Drain the carrots and
toss them in the dressing. Arrange the onion rings on a platter or individual plates
and spoon the carrots on top.

Fennel and Pomegranate Salad

Serves 6

*Pomegranates are at their best in the middle of winter, and are perfect
for dressing this crisp, light salad which I often serve at Christmas.*

about 1¼ lb / 570 g fennel bulb(s),
    trimmed
juice of ½ lemon
1 large pomegranate

3 tbsp extra virgin olive oil
sea salt
freshly ground black pepper

Slice the fennel thinly and turn the pieces in lemon juice to keep them white.
Cut the pomegranate in half. Extract the seeds whole from one half, and put to one
side. Squeeze the other half on a lemon squeezer, and mix the juice with the olive
oil and seasoning. Stir into the fennel, add the pomegranate seeds and serve
immediately. Any green feathery fennel top can be used for garnish.

Lentil Salad

Serves 4–6

8 oz / 230 g green or Puy lentils
4–5 tbsp hazelnut oil or extra virgin
   olive oil
1–2 tbsp balsamic vinegar
salt

freshly ground black pepper
1–2 shallots, peeled and finely chopped
1–2 garlic cloves, peeled and crushed
   (optional)

Put the lentils in a saucepan, cover with water and cook until just tender. Drain if necessary. While still hot, stir in the oil and vinegar, and season lightly. Stir in the shallots and garlic, if using.

Mushroom Salad

Serves 4–6

4 tbsp extra virgin olive oil
1 lb / 455 g button or cup
   mushrooms, wiped and sliced
2 tbsp good red or white wine

thinly pared rind of ½ lemon, lime or
   orange
½ tsp coriander seeds
1 small onion, peeled and thinly sliced

Heat half the olive oil in a frying pan and quickly stir-fry the mushrooms for no more than 1 minute. Remove from the heat, and transfer to a flat serving dish. Blend the rest of the oil with the wine, and pour it over the hot mushrooms. Stir in the lemon rind and the coriander seeds. Add the onion and allow to cool before serving. The hot mushrooms absorb the flavour of the wine and olive oil and give off their own juices to form a delicious dressing.

Orange, Onion and Olive Salad

Serves 4–6

This salad would make an excellent starter to a meal of Mediterranean or Moroccan flavours, including such dishes as couscous (see pages 60 and 68).

2–3 navel oranges
2 mild onions, peeled and thinly
   sliced
2–3 tbsp extra virgin olive oil

1 tbsp orange juice
salt
freshly ground black pepper
black olives

Peel the oranges, carefully removing all the white pith, and slice them thinly. Arrange alternating slices of orange and onion on a large serving platter. Sprinkle over the olive oil and orange juice, season to taste, and scatter on a handful of black olives.

Onion Salad

Serves 4–6

This is based on a recipe by Peter Grahame, originally to accompany cheese dishes, such as fondue. The contrast is perfect.

4 large sweet onions, peeled and
   thinly sliced
4 tbsp walnut oil
1 tsp sherry vinegar
2 tsp strong Dijon mustard

1 tbsp very dry white wine, such as
   Muscadet
pinch of salt
freshly ground black pepper

Put the onions in a bowl, and cover them with lightly salted boiling water. Leave for a few minutes, and then drain well. Mix the rest of the ingredients, and stir in the onions while still hot. Allow to cool in the dressing and serve.

Pear and Herb Salad with Raspberry Dressing

Serves 6

*Based on a Castelvetro recipe, this comes from our friends the
Lancellotis. Chervil, tarragon, salad burnet, chives, flat leaf parsley,
and basil are the herbs I like to use.*

6 ripe conference pears
juice of ½ lemon
6 tbsp raspberries, thawed if frozen
herbs
1 tbsp balsamic vinegar

1 tbsp extra virgin olive oil
salt
freshly ground black pepper
salad leaves

Peel, core and slice the pears, and sprinkle them with lemon juice. Rub the
raspberries through a sieve, and mix the purée with the pears. Strip the leaves of
the herbs from their stems, shred or leave whole as appropriate, and mix with the
pears. Stir in the balsamic vinegar, olive oil and seasoning. Line a large bowl with
salad leaves, heap the pear salad in the middle, and garnish with more fresh herbs
and edible flowers if you wish.

Cucumber and Mint Salad

Serves 4

2 cucumbers
1 tbsp sea salt
2 heaped tbsp thick plain yoghurt
½ tsp chilli paste, or to taste

2–3 garlic cloves, peeled and crushed
1 tbsp chopped fresh mint
mint leaves, to garnish

Peel the cucumbers, cut them in half lengthways, and scoop out and discard the
seeds. Thinly slice the cucumber and place in a sieve set over a bowl. Sprinkle with
salt, turning the slices with a spoon to make sure that all the cucumber is well
salted. Leave it to disgorge its juices for 4–5 hours, or even overnight. A great deal
of liquid will be given off. Rinse the cucumber thoroughly, and dry it well in a

clean tea-towel. Mix the cucumber into the yoghurt with the chilli paste, garlic and chopped mint and leave it to stand for 30–40 minutes before serving in order for the flavours to blend. Garnish with mint leaves.

Variations ∽ Omit the chilli paste and mint, use 4 garlic cloves and 8 tablespoons yoghurt, and stir in a handful of finely chopped, mixed, fresh herbs.

Mix the prepared cucumber slices with 2 tablespoons finely chopped chives, 1 tablespoon finely chopped fresh dill and a light dressing of extra virgin olive oil, lemon juice and a little sugar and freshly ground black pepper to taste.

Dice, rather than slice, the cucumber, disgorge as above, and then mix with an equal quantity of diced melon (watermelon would give a nice colour contrast). Sprinkle with a little sugar and freshly ground white pepper, and stir in 4 tablespoons thick plain yoghurt and 1 tablespoon white wine vinegar.

Salad Elona is a classic mixture of sliced cucumber (prepared as above) and sliced strawberries, arranged in alternating concentric circles, seasoned with freshly ground white pepper, and sprinkled with balsamic vinegar and a little extra virgin olive oil.

Grilled or Roasted Pepper Salad

Serves 6

1½ lb / 680 g red, green or yellow
  peppers
2–3 garlic cloves, peeled
½ tsp salt

freshly ground black pepper
extra virgin olive oil
sherry vinegar
2 oz / 60 g pinenuts, toasted (*optional*)

Quarter the peppers and remove the seeds, pith and stalks. Char the peppers by grilling or roasting, and then peel off the blackened skin. Put to one side. Crush the garlic in a bowl with the salt. Add the pepper and then the olive oil and vinegar to make a dressing to your taste. Stir in the peppers, and let them stand at room temperature for at least 30 minutes to absorb the flavours of the dressing. Scatter with pinenuts before serving, if liked. If you prepare this salad well in advance and refrigerate it, remember to bring it to room temperature before serving.

Variation ∽ You may add a few thin slices of mild onion and a sprinkling of crushed garlic instead of the pinenuts, if you wish.

Salad of Peas and Beans

Serves 8

some of the following, about 2 lb /
  900 g prepared weight in all:

Fresh
French beans, topped and tailed
runner beans, topped, tailed and
  sliced
broad beans, shelled
garden peas, podded
mangetout, topped and tailed
sugar snap peas, topped and tailed

Dried
green lentils, cooked and drained
chick peas, soaked, cooked and drained
flageolets, soaked, cooked and drained
soissons, haricot or cannellini beans,
  soaked, cooked and drained

2 garlic cloves, peeled and crushed
sea salt
freshly ground black pepper
juice of ½ lemon
2½ fl oz / 70 ml walnut oil

Cook the fresh vegetables as briefly as possible and drain them. In a large salad
bowl, mix the garlic, seasoning, lemon juice and oil. Stir in the freshly cooked
green vegetables and the pulses.

Coleslaw

Serves 6–8

*This is best mixed with an authentic salad cream made as described
here. If you prefer it, however, you can use mayonnaise or a yoghurt
or soured cream dressing.*

8 oz / 230 g red cabbage
8 oz / 230 g white winter cabbage
2 carrots
2 celery stalks
2 shallots or 1 medium onion
1 Cox's apple
2 tsp lemon juice
1–2 tbsp finely chopped
  parsley

Salad Cream
1 tsp caster sugar
1 tsp mild olive oil
1 tsp salt
scant tsp mustard powder
1 hard-boiled egg yolk
1 tbsp wine vinegar
7 fl oz / 200 ml single cream
2–3 tbsp milk

Cut the central stems out, and finely shred the cabbages. Peel and grate or shred the carrots. Trim and thinly slice the celery. Peel and finely chop the shallots or onion. Peel, core and chop the apple, and mix with the lemon juice. Mix all the ingredients together with the parsley, and then stir in some mayonnaise, a yoghurt or soured cream dressing or some authentic salad cream.

To make authentic salad cream mix the first four ingredients to a smooth paste. Sieve the egg yolk into the mixture, and blend well. Stir in the vinegar. Set the bowl over a pan of simmering water, and gradually add the cream and milk, stirring with a wooden spoon until the mixture lightly coats the back of the spoon. Cool and refrigerate until required.

Salade Huguette

Serves 4

8 oz / 230 g asparagus	2 Little Gem lettuces, washed
8 oz / 230 g French beans	2 hard-boiled eggs, finely chopped
4 artichoke bottoms	chopped chervil, chives or parsley
salt	mayonnaise or vinaigrette, to serve
freshly ground black pepper	

Trim the tough ends off the asparagus, and use the tender parts and the tips only. Break each stem into two or three pieces. Top and tail the beans. Ideally the three vegetables should be cooked separately, just for a few minutes until barely tender for the beans and asparagus, and longer for the artichoke bottoms, which should be quite tender but not breaking up. Drain the vegetables and season lightly. Slice the artichoke bottoms. Separate the outer leaves from the lettuces, and use them to line a salad bowl. Pile the vegetables in the middle, and place the two lettuce hearts on either side. Scatter with chopped hard-boiled egg and herbs, and serve the dressing separately.

Potato and Wild Mushroom Salad

Serves 4

8 oz / 230 g waxy potatoes
4 oz / 110 g chanterelle, shiitake or
  oyster mushrooms

3–4 tbsp extra virgin olive oil
2 shallots, peeled and finely chopped
2 tbsp sherry vinegar

Peel, boil and drain the potatoes. Cut them into approximately ½ in / 1 cm cubes, and place in a serving bowl. Clean the mushrooms, and fry them lightly in the olive oil for about 5 minutes. Add to the potatoes in the bowl. Sprinkle on the chopped shallots and the sherry vinegar, mix well, and serve.

Couscous Salad

Serves 4–6

8 oz / 230 g couscous
¼ pt / 140 ml water
6 spring onions, trimmed and finely
  sliced
3 firm, ripe tomatoes, peeled,
  deseeded and diced
12 black olives, pitted and halved
1 tbsp shredded mint leaves

1 tbsp finely chopped coriander or
  parsley
2–3 garlic cloves, peeled and crushed
3 tbsp extra virgin olive oil
2 tsp lemon or lime juice
salt
freshly ground black pepper

Put the couscous in a bowl, and sprinkle most of the water over it. As it begins to swell and dry, break up the lumps with your fingers. Add a little more water if necessary. Stir the spring onions, tomatoes, olives, herbs, garlic, olive oil and lemon or lime juice into the couscous. Season to taste and serve.

Variation ∾ A salad of bulgar wheat can be made in the same way.

Chick Pea and Vegetable Salad

Serves 4–6

4 small courgettes
4 oz / 110 g green beans, topped
   and tailed
4 oz / 110 g broccoli florets
8 spring onions, trimmed and
   chopped
2–3 garlic cloves, peeled and
   crushed

4 tbsp extra virgin olive oil
2 tsp balsamic or sherry vinegar
2 tsp finely chopped parsley
8 oz / 230 g cooked chick peas
salt
freshly ground black pepper

Bring a saucepan of water to the boil. Trim the ends off the courgettes, and break the beans into pieces, if necessary. Drop them and the broccoli into the boiling water, bring back to the boil, and simmer for 3 minutes. Drain and mix while still hot with the onions, garlic, oil, vinegar and parsley. Allow to stand for 30–45 minutes, then mix with the chick peas, and season to taste before serving.

Warm Leek and Courgette Salad

Serves 4

8 oz / 230 g baby leeks
8 oz / 230 g baby courgettes
6 tbsp walnut oil
1 tbsp wine vinegar or cider vinegar

1 garlic clove, peeled and crushed
sea salt
freshly ground black pepper
about 4 oz / 110 g salad leaves

Wash and trim the leeks and courgettes and drop them into a large saucepan of boiling salted water. Bring back to the boil and hold there for 3 minutes. Meanwhile, make a dressing with the oil, vinegar, garlic, salt and pepper. Drain the vegetables, put them in a bowl and while they are still hot, pour over the dressing and mix well. Arrange the salad leaves on individual plates and place the leeks and courgettes on top. Serve at once.

Variation ∽ Prepare a warm baby carrot and baby sweetcorn salad in the same way, but cook the carrots first for 5 minutes or so, before adding the sweetcorn and cooking the two together for a further 2–3 minutes.

Radicchio and Parmesan Salad

Serves 6

This will do duty as a starter, as a salad to follow a main course or as part of a cheese course.

2–3 heads of radicchio, depending on size	3–4 tbsp extra virgin olive oil
4 oz / 110 g Parmesan cheese	sea salt
	freshly ground black pepper

Remove any wilted or damaged leaves from the radicchio, and then take off all the leaves and wash and dry them, first in a salad spinner and then on kitchen paper. Arrange the leaves on plates. With a sharp knife or special cutter, shave the cheese into the finest slices possible, and lay them on top of the leaves. Trickle olive oil over the cheese, and then sprinkle with salt and pepper. Serve immediately.

White Root Salad

Serves 8

A cool, crisp, pale contrast, this salad is a perfect dish to follow a spicy main dish, such as a vegetable curry.

8 oz / 230 g mooli (white radish)	6 tbsp cream or plain yoghurt
8 oz / 230 g celeriac	1 garlic clove, peeled and crushed
8 oz / 230 g young parsnips	½ tsp ground cumin
8 oz / 230 g fennel	coarse sea salt
lemon juice	
2 tbsp Dijon mustard	

Peel the vegetables, then slice them and cut them into fine shreds. As you deal with each piece, drop it into a bowl of salted water with lemon juice added to stop it becoming discoloured. Mix the mustard, cream or yoghurt, garlic and cumin. Drain the vegetables thoroughly and mix with the dressing. Sprinkle coarse sea salt on top and serve immediately. It is best to make this salad just before required so that the vegetables will not be in the water too long, thus losing much of their flavour, texture and nutrients.

Warm Green Bean, Garlic and Potato Salad

Serves 4–6

1 lb / 455 g new potatoes, scrubbed
2–3 heads of garlic, cloves
   separated and peeled
8 oz / 230 g slim green beans,
   topped and tailed
4 tbsp extra virgin olive oil

sea salt
freshly ground black pepper
sherry vinegar, balsamic vinegar or wine
   vinegar
basil leaves

Drop the new potatoes into a large saucepan of boiling, lightly salted water. Add the garlic after 5 minutes. Add the beans after another minute or so. Bring everything back to the boil and simmer until the vegetables are just tender. Drain and toss in the olive oil. Season with salt and pepper, and add a little vinegar. Tear the basil leaves, and stir these into the salad. Serve warm or tepid, either in a large bowl or heaped on individual plates.

Bread and Tomato Salad

Serves 4–6

12 oz / 340 g white or wholemeal
   bread, in one piece
2–4 tbsp sherry vinegar
4 tbsp iced water
1 lb / 455 g firm, sweet, ripe
   tomatoes, peeled, quartered and
   deseeded
2–3 garlic cloves, peeled and
   crushed

½ tsp coarse sea salt
freshly ground black pepper
2½ fl oz / 70 ml extra virgin olive oil
few spring onions, trimmed and sliced
flat leaf parsley *or* basil leaves, shredded,
   to garnish

Tear the bread into bite-sized pieces and spread on a baking sheet. Place in the oven at 150°C / 300°F / Mark 2 for a few minutes or until slightly crisped. Put the bread in a bowl with the vinegar, water, tomatoes and garlic. Mix well and season with salt and pepper. Stir in the oil and leave to stand for 30–40 minutes to let the flavours develop. Sprinkle with the onions and garnish with herbs before serving.

Grilled Aubergine, Onion and Pepper Salad with Warm Garlic and Pinenut Cream

Serves 4

1–2 aubergines
¼ pt / 140 ml extra virgin olive oil
1 large mild onion
1 lb / 455 g green, red and yellow
 peppers
salad leaves (*optional*)
coarse sea salt

freshly ground black pepper
1–2 tbsp sherry vinegar
herbs, to garnish
3 oz / 85 g peeled garlic cloves
7 fl oz / 200 ml milk
1 oz / 30 g toasted pinenuts

Slice the aubergines lengthways, and brush liberally with olive oil. Peel the onion and slice into four even slices. Brush with oil. Quarter and deseed the peppers and brush with oil. Under a hot grill or in a heavy cast-iron frying pan, cook the vegetables until nicely charred and tender, turning them frequently to stop them burning. Peel the skin from the peppers. Arrange the vegetables on individual plates or on a serving platter, with salad leaves if you wish. Sprinkle with half the remaining olive oil, salt, pepper and the sherry vinegar, and garnish with herbs. Meanwhile, simmer the garlic cloves in the milk. When soft, blend them to a purée with the toasted pinenuts, a tablespoon of milk and the remaining olive oil. Spoon into a bowl and serve with the vegetables.

SIDE DISHES

Spiced Red Cabbage

Serves 6–8

1 firm red cabbage, shredded
2 onions, preferably red, peeled and
  sliced
2 crisp, sharp eating apples, peeled,
  cored and sliced
4 tbsp muscovado sugar
4 tbsp sherry vinegar
7 fl oz / 200 ml red wine

6 cloves
2 in / 5 cm cinnamon stick
1 in / 2.5 cm fresh root ginger, peeled
2 bay leaves
4 tbsp olive oil
salt
freshly ground black pepper

Layer the cabbage, onions and apples in a large ovenproof dish or casserole, sprinkling with sugar, vinegar and red wine as you go. Tuck the spices and bay leaves in the middle of the dish, and pour the olive oil on top. Cover and cook in the oven at 170°C / 325°F / Mark 3 for 2–3 hours. Add the seasoning about 30 minutes before the end of the cooking time.

Sweet and Sour Cabbage

Serves 4

2 oz / 60 g butter
1 lb / 455 g white cabbage,
  shredded

1 tbsp brown sugar
2 tbsp fruit vinegar or sherry vinegar

Heat the butter in a heavy frying pan or wok. Stir in the cabbage, and after a minute or so, add the brown sugar. Cook a little longer and then add the vinegar. Raise the heat, and stir vigorously for 20 seconds. Serve while the cabbage is still slightly crunchy and with the pan juices poured over it.

Lemon-Glazed Carrots

Serves 4

*Marmalade makes an excellent glaze with plenty of flavour of its own
to add a subtle bitter-sweet taste. Try lemon marmalade with carrots,
orange marmalade with parsnips or beetroots and lime marmalade
with turnips or swedes.*

1 lb / 455 g carrots	salt
1 oz / 30 g butter	freshly ground white pepper
1–2 tbsp lemon marmalade	1 tbsp finely chopped chives or parsley

Peel or scrub the carrots, as appropriate. Slice them, cut them into batons or
leave whole, depending on size. Put them in a saucepan with 1 in / 2.5 cm water
and simmer gently until almost tender. Stir in the butter, marmalade and seasoning
and raise the heat. Allow the cooking juices to amalgamate to a glaze, then transfer
to a serving dish. Sprinkle with herbs before serving.

Broad Beans and Peas with
Cream and Lettuce

Serves 4–6

1–2 shallots, peeled and finely chopped	3 fl oz / 85 ml single cream
1 oz / 30 g butter	finely chopped basil or summer savory
1 Little Gem lettuce, shredded	finely chopped parsley
8 oz / 230 g shelled peas	salt
8 oz / 230 g shelled broad beans	freshly ground black pepper

Cook the shallots in the butter in a saucepan without browning them. When
they are soft and translucent, stir in the lettuce. Add the peas and beans and a
splash of boiling water, no more than 2 tablespoons. Cook the vegetables for 2–3
minutes over a high heat, then add the cream, herbs and seasoning to taste. Stock
can be used in place of cream, if preferred; in which case, do not add water but
simply the boiling stock.

Celeriac with Lime

Serves 4–6

*The preparation of this dish is a little time-consuming, but the end
result is worth it.*

1 lime with a good skin	salt
1 lb / 455 g celeriac	freshly ground white pepper
2–3 oz / 60–85 g unsalted butter	

Carefully pare the zest only from the lime, and slice this into fine shreds. Peel
the celeriac, cut it into thin strips, and slice each into fine shreds. Gently cook the
celeriac in the butter for 2–3 minutes, just to blanch it and heat it through. Season
it lightly, stir in the lime zest, and heat it through so that the essential oils are
released to flavour the celeriac.

Onions in Red Wine

Serves 4

3 tbsp olive oil or a mixture of olive	7 fl oz / 200 ml red wine
oil and butter	salt
16–20 small or 4 medium-sized	freshly ground black pepper
onions, peeled	pinch of chopped thyme or rosemary
2 tsp brown sugar	chopped parsley

Butter an ovenproof dish. Heat half the olive oil, or oil and butter, in a frying
pan and cook the whole onions for a few minutes until lightly golden all over. Add
the sugar and stir until melted. Transfer the onions to the ovenproof dish. Deglaze
the pan with the wine, and pour it on the onions. Season with salt, pepper and
herbs. Sprinkle the remaining oil over the top of the onions. Cover with a lid or foil
and bake in the oven at 170°C / 325°F / Mark 3 for 40 minutes–1 hour, depending
on the size of the onions.

Baste the onions with their juices and sprinkle with parsley. Serve straight from
the ovenproof dish.

Glazed Chestnuts

Serves 6–8

1 lb / 455 g chestnuts, peeled
1 pt / 570 ml vegetable stock or
   fruity white wine

1–2 oz / 30–60 g butter
1 oz / 30 g light muscovado sugar

Cook the chestnuts in the stock or wine until tender. Drain them, reserving the cooking liquid for soup or stock for another dish. Return the chestnuts to the pan with the butter and sugar, cover and set over a low heat until the sugar has dissolved. Shake to glaze the chestnuts.

Baked Jerusalem Artichokes

Serves 4

The following recipe makes an interesting change from potatoes.

2 lb / 900 g Jerusalem artichokes
½ pt / 280 ml thin béchamel sauce
   or cream

1 oz / 30 g butter
salt
freshly ground black pepper

This may seem a large quantity for four people, but because of all the knobbly bits, there is often quite a lot of waste with Jerusalem artichokes. I find that if you scrub them well, cutting off any bruised knobs, it is not necessary to peel them. Since making this discovery, I serve Jerusalem artichokes often in the autumn and winter. I love their nutty flavour. Cut the vegetables into ¼ in / 0.5 cm slices and drop into a large pan of boiling water. Simmer for 2–3 minutes. Drain and layer them in a buttered baking dish with the béchamel sauce and seasoning, finishing with a layer of sauce on top. Bake for 25–30 minutes at 200°C / 400°F / Mark 6.

Patatas Alioli
(Potatoes with Garlic and Olive Oil)

Serves 6–8

4 garlic cloves, peeled
¼–½ tsp salt, to taste
¼ pt / 140 ml olive oil

lemon juice, to taste
1 lb / 455 g new potatoes, boiled and
  diced

Have all your ingredients at room temperature. Pound the garlic in a mortar until it becomes a fine paste. Adding a pinch of salt at the beginning will help give the garlic a 'grip' in the mortar. Add the oil slowly but constantly, stirring all the time until the sauce thickens. Mix the lemon juice with a few drops of water and add to the sauce with more salt if necessary. Mix with the potatoes and serve. If the sauce separates rather than emulsifies, it still tastes very good.

Steamed Chinese Leaves and Mangetout

Serves 6

1 head of Chinese leaves
3 oz / 85 g mangetout
2 star anise

Dressing
2 tbsp toasted sesame oil
2 tbsp soy sauce
2 tbsp brown sugar
2 tbsp rice vinegar

Remove any damaged outer leaves from the Chinese leaves. Top and tail the mangetout. Shred the leaves across and mix them with the mangetout. Place them in a steamer basket with the star anise buried in the middle. Steam for 5 minutes. Meanwhile, mix together the ingredients for the dressing and pour it into a serving bowl. Drain the vegetables and toss in the dressing while still hot.

Stewed Cucumbers

Serves 6

2 onions
2 cucumbers
3 oz / 85 g unsalted butter,
  softened
2 tsp plain flour
6 tbsp vegetable stock

2 tbsp white wine
1 blade of mace or pinch of
  ground mace
salt
freshly ground white pepper

Peel and thinly slice the onions. Cut the cucumbers in half lengthways, scoop out the seeds, and then slice the cucumber halves. Melt 2 oz / 60 g butter in a frying pan, and mix the rest with the flour to make *beurre manié*. Fry the onion in the melted butter for a few minutes until wilted, and then add the cucumber. Fry together for a few minutes more. Add the stock, wine and mace, then gradually stir in the *beurre manié* in small pieces. Shake the pan, then let all the ingredients stew together for a few minutes. Season and serve.

Deep-fried Leeks

Serves 6

1½ lb / 680 g leeks
groundnut (peanut) or sunflower oil for frying

Trim the leeks, and remove the coarse tops and outer skin. Cut into 3 in / 7.5 cm lengths, and slice in half lengthways. Shred the leeks into long, thin strips. Rinse and dry them thoroughly. Put oil in a wok or deep frying pan to a depth of about 3 in / 7.5 cm, and heat until a cube of bread sizzles as soon as it is dropped in. Fry the leeks in batches for about 20 seconds each, and drain them on kitchen paper before serving.

Creamed Leeks

Serves 4–6

1½ lb / 680 g leeks
knob of butter

butter, single cream or crème fraîche, to
    mix
freshly grated nutmeg

Trim the leeks, and remove the coarse tops and outer skin. Cut into very thin slices and wash thoroughly. Dry on kitchen paper. Put the leeks in a heavy saucepan with a knob of butter, cover with a lid, and cook gently until the leeks are tender. Use a fork to mash the leeks to a purée, adding a little more butter or some cream or crème fraîche. Add a little grated nutmeg, and serve.

Variation ∾ Brussels sprouts can be prepared in the same way.

Stir-fried Greens with Preserved Ginger and Sesame Seeds

Serves 6

1 lb / 455 g spring greens
½ head of Chinese leaves
1 lb / 455 g spinach
½ in / 1 cm fresh root ginger,
    peeled
2–3 garlic cloves, peeled
1 star anise
2–3 tbsp groundnut (peanut) oil
4 spring onions, trimmed and thinly
    sliced

1–2 tbsp soy sauce
1 tbsp rice wine
1 tbsp rice wine vinegar
2–3 pieces of preserved ginger, thinly
    sliced
2 tsp toasted sesame oil
1 tbsp toasted sesame seeds

Wash, trim and shred the vegetables, keeping them in separate piles. Fry the fresh ginger, garlic and star anise in the oil in a wok or large frying pan for 4–5 minutes. Discard the seasonings, and put the spring greens into the hot oil. Stir-fry for 2–3 minutes before adding the Chinese leaves. After stir-frying for 2–3 minutes, add the spinach and spring onions. When the spinach has collapsed, add the soy sauce, wine, vinegar and preserved ginger. Cover with a lid and steam for a few minutes more. Stir in the sesame oil, and then serve scattered with sesame seeds.

Roast New Potatoes and Garlic

Serves 4

4 heads of garlic
extra virgin olive oil

1 lb / 455 g new potatoes, scrubbed
　and pricked
coarse sea salt

Peel the outer skin from the garlic heads, but leave them whole. Slice a cap off the top, brush with olive oil and replace. Oil a roasting tin, and put in the garlic and new potatoes, sprinkling with a little salt. Roast in a preheated oven at 180°C / 350°F / Mark 4 until both are tender. To eat, break cloves off the garlic, and squeeze the soft flesh out of the skin to eat with the potatoes.

Variation ～ Bake the scrubbed potatoes with peeled whole cloves of garlic and a little olive oil and seasoning in foil-wrapped parcels. This should take about 40 minutes at 180°C / 350°F / Mark 4. Put 4–5 potatoes and 2 large garlic cloves in each parcel.

Fried Puffballs

This is one of my favourite wild mushroom recipes; quantities are not given because who knows how many you will find?

puffballs
eggs
milk
nutmeg

flour
salt
freshly ground
　black pepper

paprika
butter
olive oil
finely chopped parsley

Peel and slice the puffballs about ¼ in/0.5 cm thick. Beat the eggs, milk and nutmeg in a shallow dish, as if you were making French toast. Sift the flour, salt, pepper and paprika on to a plate. Heat a mixture of butter and olive oil in a frying pan. Dip the puffball slices into the egg mixture, then into the flour, and finally into the egg mixture once more. Fry the slices in a single layer, turning them once. Serve sprinkled with parsley.

Variation ～ If you have only a small harvest of puffballs, say one or two, peel and dice them, cook as described above, and use them in place of croûtons in a bowl of salad greens, or mix them with other mushrooms into a bowl of freshly made pasta.

Marinated Mushrooms

It is a curious fact that mushrooms, which contain a lot of water,
actually give up some of their moisture when quickly boiled in water.
I suggest cooking them in a mixture of water and wine, which will
produce an excellent mushroom broth that can be used as a base for
mushroom soups.

2 lb / 900 g fresh mushrooms
¾ pt / 430 ml good dry white wine
¾ pt / 430 ml water
4 tbsp white wine vinegar
2 bay leaves
1 tbsp peppercorns
1 small cinnamon stick

1 tsp sea salt
3 in / 7.5 cm strip of orange zest
¼ pt / 140 ml good olive oil
salt
freshly ground black pepper
chopped parsley, to garnish

Wipe the mushrooms carefully, and trim off the bases of the stems. Put the rest
of the ingredients, except the olive oil, seasoning and 1 tablespoon wine vinegar,
into a large saucepan. Bring to the boil, and simmer for 5 minutes. Put the
mushrooms into the pan, bring back to the boil, and simmer for 6–7 minutes.
Strain the liquid into a bowl and reserve for soup. Drain the mushrooms, then dry
them by placing them on several layers of kitchen paper or an absorbent tea-towel.
When dry, put them into a serving bowl with the olive oil and the remaining wine
vinegar. Season to taste, and garnish with the chopped parsley.

Creamed Turnips

2 lb / 900 g turnips
3 oz / 85 g unsalted butter
6 oz / 170 g crème fraîche or soured
   cream

salt
freshly ground white pepper

Scrub the turnips and boil until tender. Peel, and put in a food processor with
half the butter and cream. Process, and gradually add the rest of the butter and
cream. Season to taste and reheat gently if necessary.

Variation ∽ Use 1 lb / 455 g turnips and 1 lb / 455 g potatoes.

Grilled Radicchio

Serves 4

This is good served with a sprinkling of sea salt, a little more olive oil, and a splash of lemon juice or balsamic vinegar.

14–16 oz / 395–455 g radicchio,   salt
  2 firm round heads   freshly ground black pepper
4–6 tbsp good olive oil

Remove any bruised or wilted leaves and roots from the radicchio. Wash the heads and cut into quarters. Brush each piece with olive oil, season lightly and place under a moderate grill until cooked through, turning occasionally.

Variations ∾ Grill lettuce in the same way. Use a firm, crisp lettuce, and, in addition to the olive oil and seasoning, sprinkle the cut surfaces with crushed garlic and grated cheese (Gruyère, Parmesan and Cheddar are good), before grilling.

Aubergines, courgettes, pepper and potatoes are all good grilled. Slice the aubergines and courgettes lengthways, brush each slice with olive oil, season, and grill on both sides. Quarter and deseed peppers, oil and season, and again grill on both sides, removing the skin as it peels off. Parboil, drain and dry potatoes before brushing with oil, seasoning and grilling on both sides. If the potatoes are large, slice them after parboiling.

Aligot
(Cheese and Potato Purée)

Serves 4–6

Here is another favourite dish, from Central France, that will send welcoming smells from the kitchen in the winter; I do not feel it is a summer dish. The traditional recipe used butter and cream. However, olive oil and thick Greek yoghurt make excellent substitutes.

2 lb / 900 g potatoes, scrubbed   8 oz / 230 g Gruyère, Lancashire or,
4 oz / 110 g butter *or* 4 fl oz / 115 ml   traditionally, Cantal cheese, grated
  extra virgin olive oil   salt
4 tbsp cream or yoghurt   freshly ground black pepper

Boil the potatoes until tender, then drain. When cool enough to handle, scoop out the cooked potato into a saucepan and mash until smooth. With a wooden spoon, beat in the butter or oil, keeping the pan over a low heat. Stir in the cream or yoghurt, and then add the cheese, stirring until it has melted into the potatoes. Season to taste and serve immediately.

Aloo Gobi Subji
(Dry-cooked Potato and Cauliflower)

Serves 4–6

3–4 tsp ghee or concentrated butter
1 onion, peeled and finely chopped
1–2 fresh green chillies, deseeded
  and chopped
1 in / 2.5 cm fresh root ginger,
  peeled and chopped
1 tsp ground turmeric
1 tsp salt

1 lb / 455 g medium potatoes, peeled
  and quartered
1 medium cauliflower, broken into
  florets
1 tbsp coriander seeds, crushed
1–2 tsp garam masala
1 tbsp coriander leaves, shredded

Melt the ghee or butter in a heavy saucepan or flameproof casserole, add the onion, chillies and ginger, and fry until the onion begins to brown. Stir in the turmeric, cook for 1–2 minutes, and then add the salt and potatoes. Cook, stirring frequently, for about 10 minutes. If the potatoes show signs of sticking, add 1–2 tablespoons water, but avoid this if possible as the potatoes will become mushy. Add the cauliflower florets, and cook for a further 15–20 minutes or until the cauliflower is tender. Add the coriander seeds, and stir into the mixture. Sprinkle on the garam masala and the coriander leaves. Check the seasoning, stir and serve.

With a dry subji like this, it is a good idea to serve something wet, such as a dal or lentil curry.

Braised Chicory

Serves 4

*When choosing chicory, look for tightly furled heads, just tinged at the
tips of the leaves with yellow.*

1½ lb / 680 g chicory
1 tbsp wine vinegar or lemon juice
salt
1 oz / 30 g unsalted butter

up to ¼ pt / 140 ml vegetable stock,
 white wine or water
freshly ground black pepper
freshly grated nutmeg
1 tbsp finely chopped parsley

Remove any browning leaves from the chicory, and cut a thin slice off the
bottom of each root. Bring a pan of water to the boil with the vinegar or lemon
juice and 1 teaspoon salt. Put in the chicory and simmer for 5 minutes. Drain and
dry on kitchen paper. Melt the butter in a frying pan and cook the chicory in it
very gently, moistening from time to time by adding a little stock, wine or water.
When the vegetables are tender, put them in a heated serving dish. Boil up the
cooking juices together with any remaining stock, wine or water. Season with salt,
pepper and nutmeg, and pour over the chicory. Sprinkle parsley on top before
serving.

Dhal

Serves 4–6

1 onion, peeled and thinly sliced
1 tbsp oil
2 tsp cumin seeds, ground
1 tsp coriander seeds, ground

2–3 cloves, ground
8 oz / 230 g red lentils
1 pt / 570 ml water
salt

Fry the onion in the oil in a saucepan until wilted, and then add the spices, and
fry for a few minutes. Stir in the lentils, and when they are coated with oil and
spices, add most of the water. Bring to the boil, cover and simmer until the lentils
are almost tender. Add salt at this stage and the rest of the water. If you prefer a
soupy dhal, add a further ¼ pt / 140 ml water.

Mint Sambol

Serves 4–6

1 oz / 30 g mint leaves
4 black peppercorns
½ tsp coarse sea salt
½ tsp sugar
1–2 fresh green chillies, deseeded
   and chopped

3–4 garlic cloves, peeled and chopped
2 tbsp toasted desiccated coconut
lime juice, to taste

Put the mint leaves, peppercorns, salt and sugar in a mortar, and pound to a paste. Add the chillies and garlic, and pound until well mixed. Scrape into a bowl, mix in the coconut and stir in lime juice to taste.

Variation ✀ Omit the peppercorns, replace the garlic with one finely chopped shallot, add a tablespoon of ground almonds, and instead of just the mint, use a mixture of chopped fresh leaves, chosen from chives, coriander leaves, parsley, mint, watercress and rocket.

Basmati Rice

(cooked by the absorption method)

Serves 4

This is the best method for cooking rice to accompany curries.

1 small onion, peeled and finely
   chopped
2 tbsp ghee or clarified butter
1 tsp salt
2 tbsp ground cumin

4 cloves and the seeds of 3 cardamom
   pods
10 oz / 280 g basmati rice
1 pt / 570 ml water

Fry the onion in the ghee or butter in a heavy saucepan, and when golden brown, add the salt and spices. Continue frying for a few minutes, without burning. Stir in the rice until well coated with the ghee or butter. Pour in the water, bring to the boil, cover with a tight-fitting lid, and cook over the lowest heat possible for 30 minutes, or in a preheated oven at 180°C / 350°F / Mark 4 for about 25 minutes.

Bulgar Wheat

Serves 4

Cracked wheat, burghul and pourgouri are other names for this very good cereal. It makes a good accompaniment to vegetable curries as a change from rice.

1 tbsp olive oil
1 small onion, peeled and thinly
　sliced
6 oz / 170 g bulgar wheat

6 fl oz / 170 ml water or stock
pinch of salt
herbs, such as flat-leaved parsley,
　coriander or mint

Heat the oil in a heavy saucepan, and gently fry the onion for about 10 minutes until it is soft and brown but not burnt. Stir in the bulgar wheat until it is well coated with oil. Pour on the water or stock, add the salt, bring to the boil, cover and turn the heat right down. Cook for about 20 minutes or until the wheat is tender and has absorbed all the liquid. Serve sprinkled with herbs.

Main Dishes

The recipes in this chapter are for substantial vegetarian dishes based on vegetables, pasta, rice, grains, pulses, eggs and cheese and they ably demonstrate the compatibility of vegetables with each other, and not just as accompaniments. Many dishes here are suitable for everyday meals while other, more time-consuming recipes, are best reserved for entertaining.

Pasta is an inexpensive, comforting, homely food, and one of the best ingredients available for cooking quickly. There was a time when, if you wanted to eat good, authentic Italian pasta, you had to fly off to Milan, Bologna or Palermo. Then gradually it became possible to obtain quality Italian dried pasta outside of Italy, and now there are fresh pasta shops churning it out by the metre in every shape and colour. Do not assume that 'fresh' is best, however. Good *pasta secca*, factory-made dried Italian pasta made from hard or durum wheat, is the most convenient. Homemade pasta (see pages 110–112) is not at all difficult to make, but it is best undertaken in dry conditions, otherwise the pasta can be rather sticky to work with.

Sauces for pasta come in as great a range as pasta itself. Whilst there are no hard and fast rules about it, certain sauces are best suited to certain pasta shapes. Chunky vegetable sauces are better with the thicker, larger pasta shapes, such as *penne* and *rigatoni*, or with those which nicely enfold a sauce, such as the broad *pappardelle* or *festonati* with fluted edges.

Risotto is another classic Italian dish and consists of Italian short grain rice gently simmered and stirred until it absorbs its cooking liquid. To achieve the correct consistency, always use a good risotto rice, such as arborio. Different vegetables can be added to vary the dish as you wish (see pages 124–128).

Other dishes in this chapter are based on grains (polenta and quinoa), pulses, eggs and cheese. Some of them, such as the Spanish Omelette (see page 135), are infinitely variable and provide good, wholesome vegetarian meals, as well as being a convenient way to use up leftover vegetables. (See page 60 for information about cooking with grains.)

Asparagus and Almonds in Filo

Serves 4–6

To suggest at the beginning of the English asparagus season, which opens in early May, that you might cook and eat this silky, green delicacy, long awaited through winter and spring, any other way than quickly boiled or steamed until just tender, and then served warm, dressed in nothing more than a little good oil or butter and lemon juice, would be seen by some as sacrilege. But once the asparagus season is in full swing, the shops are full of it, and it is so easy to get carried away, buy too much, and then find it a few days later looking somewhat fridge-worn. This is a good recipe for such times.

5 oz / 140 g butter
1 onion, peeled and finely chopped
1 lb / 455 g asparagus, trimmed and blanched
4 oz / 110 g flaked almonds, toasted
6 tbsp single cream
4 oz / 110 g Cheddar cheese, grated
salt
freshly ground black pepper
5 sheets filo pastry

Make the filling first. Melt 1 oz / 30 g of the butter and fry the onion until softened. Cut the asparagus into 1 in / 2.5 cm pieces, and fry briefly with the onion without letting it colour. Remove the pan from the heat, and stir in the almonds, cream and cheese. Season to taste, and cool. Meanwhile, melt the remaining butter and preheat the oven to 200°C / 400°F / Mark 6. Lay one sheet of filo pastry on a work surface. Cover the remaining sheets with a clean, damp cloth. Brush the first sheet with melted butter and cover with a second. Brush with melted butter again, and repeat with the remaining three sheets. Spread the asparagus filling over the pastry, leaving a 1 in / 2.5 cm border around the edge. Fold in the two shorter sides and then roll up. Carefully brush with the remaining butter, and bake in the oven for 20 minutes. Turn the oven down to 180°C / 350°F / Mark 4, and cook for a further 10 minutes, until crisp and golden brown.

Honey-glazed Stilton Potatoes

Serves 4

4 large baking potatoes
2 oz / 60 g butter
freshly ground black pepper

4 oz / 110 g Blue Stilton, thinly sliced
1–2 tbsp honey

Scrub and dry the potatoes, and prick them all over. Bake towards the top of a preheated oven at 200°C / 400°F / Mark 6, until they feel soft when squeezed slightly. Cooking time will depend on the size and thickness of the potato but can be speeded up by inserting a small metal skewer into each potato at its thickest point so that heat is conducted to the centre more quickly. When cooked, remove the potatoes from the oven and cut a slice from the broadest surface of each one. Scoop the soft flesh out into a bowl, keeping the skins intact. Mix in the butter with a fork, and pepper to taste. Spoon back into the potato skins and smooth the surface, leaving enough room to lay thin slices of Stilton on top. Trickle honey over the cheese and put under a hot grill for 2–3 minutes for the honey and the cheese to melt and bubble. Serve immediately.

Artichoke and Potato Casserole

Serves 6

1 onion, peeled and thinly sliced
4 tbsp extra virgin olive oil
2½ lb / 1.10 kg new potatoes,
    scrubbed and dried
12 baby artichokes *or* 3 medium
    artichokes

12 garlic cloves, peeled
¼ pt / 140 ml dry white wine
sea salt
freshly ground black pepper
1–2 tbsp finely chopped parsley

Fry the onion gently in half the olive oil, using a flameproof casserole. Add the potatoes and fry all over, then turn down the heat, and continue to cook, partly covered, while you prepare the artichokes. Small ones just need trimming and rinsing before putting in the pan. Larger ones should be trimmed down by about a third, the outer leaves and stalk removed, and then quartered. The choke can then be pulled out. As you prepare each artichoke or piece, drop it into acidulated water to stop it discolouring. Drain the artichokes, and add to the casserole together with the garlic cloves and half the white wine. Season lightly, and simmer very gently until the vegetables are just tender, adding more wine and the remaining olive oil from time to time. Check the seasoning, scatter on the chopped parsley and serve direct from the pan.

Variation ∞ To make this into a more substantial dish, asparagus tips or freshly shelled peas can be added towards the end of the cooking time. A sprig of tarragon cooked with it gives a good flavour.

Aubergine, Okra and Tomato Stew

Serves 4–6

This rich vegetable stew has even more flavour if made the day before required and eaten cold (but not chilled) with hot pitta bread. If you like such things chilli hot, then cook a small green or red chilli in the stew but carefully remove the seeds first.

1 medium onion, peeled and sliced
2½ fl oz / 70 ml extra virgin olive
 oil
1 lb / 455 g aubergines
6 garlic cloves, peeled
8 oz / 230 g okra

1 lb / 455 g peeled tomatoes, fresh or
 canned
2 sprigs thyme
salt
freshly ground black pepper
chopped flat-leaved parsley or coriander

Fry the onion gently in some of the olive oil in a flameproof casserole until it browns. Dice the aubergines into ½ in / 1 cm chunks, and add to the pan, together with the garlic. Add more olive oil, as the aubergine absorbs it like blotting paper. Trim the okra, carefully paring away the stalk end, and add it to the pan with the tomatoes, thyme and a little salt and pepper. Cover and cook over a low heat or in a low oven for 2–3 hours, until the vegetables are soft. Towards the end of the cooking time, stir in any remaining olive oil. Before serving, hot or cold, stir in the parsley or coriander.

Cabbage Stuffed with Wild Mushrooms

Serves 4

This is a rather grand recipe for cabbage. If you can get fresh wild mushrooms, so much the better. If not, the flavour of dried wild mushrooms is an important addition and worth the extra money. Dried wild mushrooms are really quite economical, go a long way and keep well. Just one small piece of dried porcini snipped into a soup or casserole immediately enhances the flavour.

½ oz / 15 g dried wild mushrooms	1 egg
½ pt / 280 ml boiling vegetable stock	salt
	freshly ground black pepper
8 large cabbage leaves	6 juniper berries
12 oz / 340 g fresh mushrooms	sprig of rosemary
4 oz / 110 g ricotta	2–3 tbsp extra virgin olive oil
2 shallots	

Cut the dried mushrooms into small pieces, place them in a bowl, and pour on the boiling stock. Cut the hard central rib from each cabbage leaf, blanch the leaves thoroughly in boiling water, then drain. Wipe the fresh mushrooms, only peeling if absolutely necessary, and chop them very finely (I use a food processor at this point). Mix thoroughly with the ricotta. Peel and finely chop the shallots and add these to the mushroom and cheese mixture. Separate the egg. Beat the egg yolk lightly, and stir this into the mixture. Season to taste. Whisk the egg white, and fold this in. Strain the dried wild mushroom pieces, reserving the liquor, and stir them in gently.

Divide the stuffing between the eight cabbage leaves, and roll into neat parcels. Place in a lightly oiled baking dish. Scatter the juniper berries, and lay the sprig of rosemary on the cabbage parcels, and sprinkle with mushroom liquor and olive oil. Cover with foil, and bake in a preheated oven at 190°C / 375°F / Mark 5 for 25 minutes. Serve hot.

Root Vegetable and Chick Pea Curry

Serves 6–8

1 large onion, peeled and sliced
2 tbsp groundnut (peanut) or
  sunflower oil
1 tbsp ground coriander
2 tsp ground cumin
1 tsp cardamom seeds
1 tsp ground turmeric
1 tsp paprika
½ tsp chilli powder or cayenne
  pepper (or to taste)

12 oz / 340 g turnip, peeled and cubed
12 oz / 340 g celeriac, peeled and cubed
1 lb / 455 g potatoes, peeled and cubed
12 oz / 340 g chick peas, soaked and
  cooked
1 pt / 570 ml vegetable stock
4–5 sprigs coriander
2 bay leaves
salt
freshly ground black pepper

Fry the onion in the oil in a large saucepan until wilted, then add the spices and fry for a few minutes more. Add the cubed vegetables and turn them in the spices. Add the chick peas and stock. Strip the leaves from the coriander, and set aside. Put the coriander stalks and bay leaves in the pan, season, and bring to the boil. Cover and simmer on the lowest possible heat, or cook in a warm oven at 170°C / 325 °F / Mark 3, until the vegetables are tender. Stir in the coriander leaves. Serve with brown or white rice, mango chutney and thick yoghurt.

Celeriac, Pumpkin and Walnut Crumble

Serves 8

1 lb / 455 g celeriac
1 lb / 455 g pumpkin, peeled and
  deseeded
2 onions, peeled and finely chopped
2 tbsp olive oil
2 tbsp finely chopped parsley

8 oz / 230 g button mushrooms
5 oz / 140 g butter
2 oz / 60 g fresh breadcrumbs
3 tbsp finely chopped chives
3 oz / 85 g walnuts, finely chopped

Peel and slice the celeriac and blanch it immediately in lightly acidulated boiling water. Drain. Slice the pumpkin fairly thickly. Sweat the onions in the olive oil until soft, and then add the sliced vegetables. Cover with a lid, and let the vegetables 'steam' on top of the onions until tender. Transfer them to a buttered baking dish, sprinkling each layer with parsley.

Preheat the oven to 220°C / 425°F / Mark 7. Wipe and slice the mushrooms, and fry in half the butter until soft. This should be done over a high heat to evaporate the liquid. When cooked, finely chop the mushrooms. Mix them with the breadcrumbs, chives, walnuts and remaining butter, and spoon over the vegetables in the baking dish. Bake for 10–12 minutes in the top of the oven.

Variation ➣ Layer the cooked celeriac, pumpkin and onion in individual, ovenproof serving dishes, top with the mushroom, breadcrumb and walnut crumble mix, and finish off under a hot grill, rather than in the oven.

Aubergine and Okra Brown Curry

Serves 4–6

1 lb / 455 g aubergine, diced
1 medium onion, peeled and thinly
  sliced
1–2 tbsp oil
8 oz / 230 g okra
1–2 fresh green chillies, deseeded
  and chopped

2 tsp brown mustard seeds
2 tsp cumin seeds, ground
1 in / 2.5 cm cinnamon stick
1 tbsp tamarind water or lime juice
½ pt / 280 ml coconut milk
  (see below)
salt

Gently fry the aubergine and onion in the oil in a saucepan, and while these are cooking, trim the okra. Add the chillies and the rest of the spices to the pan, and cook for 5 minutes. Take care with the mustard seeds, as they pop and spit. Put in the okra and tamarind water or lime juice, mix well, and pour on half the coconut milk. Bring to the boil, and simmer until the vegetables are tender. Add more coconut milk as necessary, and add salt to taste.

Coconut Milk

Makes 1½ pt / 850 ml

Leftover coconut milk can be stored in the refrigerator for 2–3 days.
'Cream' will form on the top, which should be stirred back into the
milk before using.

1 lb/ 455 g desiccated coconut
1½ pt / 850 ml water

Put the coconut and water in a saucepan, bring to the boil, and simmer for 5 minutes. Allow to cool until you can hold your finger in it without burning. Pour through a fine sieve into a bowl, pressing out as much liquid as possible from the coconut trapped in the sieve. Cool and refrigerate until required.

Garden Curry

Serves 4–6

*Pandanus leaves are the long, thin leaves of the screw-pine tree. They
are used in Asian and oriental cooking to add a nutty flavour and
green colour to curries and other dishes. Both pandanus and curry
leaves are available from oriental food shops, though pandanus leaves
might prove harder to find.*

3 lb / 1.35 kg vegetables (include,
  for example, broccoli, peas,
  runner beans, cabbage, new
  potatoes, small carrots,
  cauliflower, kohlrabi)
1 onion, peeled and sliced
1–2 fresh green chillies, deseeded
  and chopped, to taste
2 tbsp sunflower oil
sprig of curry leaves
piece of pandanus leaf *(optional)*

1 lemon grass stalk, sliced
1 tbsp cumin seeds, ground
2 tsp coriander seeds, ground
1 tsp ground turmeric or mild curry
  powder
4 cloves
1 in / 2.5 cm cinnamon stick
¼ tsp cardamom seeds
1 pt / 570 ml vegetable stock
salt

Prepare the vegetables as necessary and break or cut into bite-sized pieces,
slices or florets. Fry the onion and chillies in the oil until softened, then add the
leaves and spices. Cook for 5 minutes, then stir in the vegetables. When well coated
with spices, add three quarters of the stock and bring to the boil. Reduce the heat,
cover and simmer until the vegetables are almost tender. Uncover, add the rest of
the stock, salt to taste, and continue cooking until done.

Mushroom and Potato Pie

Serves 4

You can make this with fresh mushrooms, but it has a richer flavour if made with a mixture of fresh and dried mushrooms. Use just one variety of dried mushroom or mix them, as you wish. They must be well soaked before cooking. I recommend pouring plenty of boiling water over them and leaving for an hour at least. Chinese flower mushrooms take longer, and I would poach them for an hour after an hour's soaking. Canned or bottled wild mushrooms can, of course, be used with no preparation.

1 lb / 455 g fresh and dried
   mushrooms, ready to use
3–4 lb / 1.35–1.80 kg potatoes
6 oz / 170 g butter

salt
freshly ground black pepper
½ pt / 280 ml stock, milk or single
   cream

Cut the mushrooms into small pieces. Peel the potatoes and slice as thinly as possible. Layer the potatoes and mushrooms in an ovenproof dish, dotting with butter and seasoning each layer of potatoes. Pour on the liquid, cover with foil, and bake in a preheated oven at 180°C / 350°F / Mark 4 for about 1 hour, less if the potatoes are wafer-thin; more if they are chunky.

Wild Greens and Barley 'Risotto'

Serves 4–6

Many of the best edible green plants grow wild in relative profusion. Use a guide book to help you identify them, and only pick what you can be absolutely certain of identifying, thus avoiding the few plants that are poisonous. Pick well away from roadside verges and recently sprayed areas. Always wash well and dry all wild greens thoroughly (see method) before cooking. The strong flavour of wild greens goes well with pasta or a grain, such as rice or barley, as in this inexpensive and sustaining dish and the crumble recipe opposite.

2 lb / 900 g freshly picked wild greens, such as nettles, dock leaves, Jack-by-the-hedge, hogweed, fat hen, alexander stems, ground elder, chickweed, wood sorrel, orach and dandelion leaves
1 small onion *or* 2 shallots, peeled and chopped

2 oz / 60 g butter
2 tbsp extra virgin olive oil
12 oz / 340 g pearl barley
½ pt / 280 ml white wine
1½ pt / 850 ml hot vegetable stock
salt
freshly ground black pepper
freshly grated Parmesan cheese

First wash the wild greens thoroughly in several changes of warm water, and then dry them on kitchen paper or in a salad spinner. Toss them into boiling water to blanch them. Tender leaves, such as chickweed, fat hen, wood sorrel, orach and Jack-by-the-hedge, will need only the briefest blanching for about 1 minute. Tougher, stronger leaves, such as dock and nettles, should be blanched for 2–3 minutes. Drain, rinse, dry thoroughly and roughly chop. Leave on one side.

Gently fry the onion or shallots in half the butter and the olive oil in a large saucepan. Stir in the barley, add half the wine, and stir until it has been absorbed. Add the remaining wine, and cook gently until that too has been absorbed. Stir in the vegetable stock, a little at a time, allowing each batch to be absorbed before adding the next. After adding two or three batches of stock, stir in the prepared greens, and continue cooking until the barley is tender and all the stock is used up. Season to taste, and just before serving, stir in the remaining butter and the Parmesan cheese.

Wild Greens and Wild Rice Crumble

Serves 4–6

*The wild greens in this recipe can be supplemented with bolted
lettuce, spinach, watercress, Swiss chard or beet or turnip tops. For
information on wild greens, see the recipe for Wild Greens and Barley
'Risotto' opposite.*

4 oz / 110 g wild rice

3 lb / 1.35 kg wild greens, such as
chickweed, fat hen, wood sorrel,
orach, Jack-by-the-hedge, nettles,
dock leaves, hogweed, alexander
stems, ground elder and
dandelion leaves

2–3 shallots or small onions, peeled
and chopped

2 tbsp extra virgin olive oil

1 tbsp finely chopped herbs, such as
thyme, marjoram and rosemary

6 oz / 170 g hard cheese, grated

4 eggs

¼ pt / 140 ml buttermilk or single cream

salt

freshly ground black pepper

2 oz / 60 g fresh breadcrumbs

2 oz / 60 g nuts, finely chopped

Put the wild rice in a saucepan with about four times its volume of water, bring
to the boil, and simmer until the rice is tender. Drain if necessary. Wash, blanch,
drain and dry the leaves, as described in the recipe for Wild Greens and Barley
'Risotto' (opposite). Place them in a large saucepan, cover and cook over a fairly
high heat, stirring frequently, until the greens have collapsed. Drain them.

Sweat the shallots or onions in the oil in a large saucepan, and then mix in the
cooked rice and greens, the herbs and most of the grated cheese. Beat the eggs with
the buttermilk or cream, and mix this thoroughly with the vegetables. Season to
taste, and spoon into an oiled ovenproof dish. Smooth the top, and sprinkle on the
remaining cheese mixed with the breadcrumbs and chopped nuts. Dot with extra
butter or oil, if you wish, and bake in a preheated oven at 180°C / 350°F / Mark 4
for about 45 minutes.

Leek, Potato and Parmesan Strudel

Serves 6

3 oz / 85 g flaked almonds
2 oz / 60 g ground almonds
6–8 oz / 170–230 g butter
12 oz / 340 g leeks (white parts
  only)
½ pt / 280 ml milk
1 bay leaf

2 cloves
1½ lb / 680 g potatoes
salt
freshly ground black pepper
4 oz / 110 g Parmesan cheese, freshly
  grated
4 sheets filo or strudel pastry

Separately fry the flaked and ground almonds in a little of the butter, and put
to one side to cool. The flakes should be crisp and golden, not brown. Peel, trim
and thinly slice the leeks. Wash thoroughly to remove any grit, shake excess water
from them, and put in a saucepan with the milk, bay leaf and cloves. Cook until the
leeks are just tender, then drain and put to one side. Reserve the milk, and discard
the bay leaf and cloves. Peel the potatoes and boil in lightly salted water. Drain,
and mash them with a little of the milk in which the leeks were cooked and some
more of the butter. Season lightly with salt and pepper, and stir in 1 oz / 30 g of the
Parmesan and the cooked leeks. Melt the remaining butter.

To assemble the dish, liberally brush each sheet of pastry with melted butter.
Lay the first sheet on top of the second, and then scatter the flaked almonds,
ground almonds and 2 oz / 60 g Parmesan over the whole surface. Lay the
remaining two buttered sheets on top. Spoon the mashed potato and leek mixture
in an even line about 2 in / 5 cm from one long edge of the pastry. Roll up
carefully, and transfer to a buttered and floured baking sheet, curving it slightly to
fit if necessary. Brush the top with the remaining melted butter, sprinkle with
Parmesan, and cook in the top half of a preheated oven at 190°C / 375°F / Mark 5
for about 40 minutes, until golden brown.

Winter Vegetable Gratin

Serves 6–8

1 lb / 455 g celeriac
1 lb / 455 g onions
1 lb / 455 g potatoes
1 lb / 455 g leeks
8 oz / 230 g fennel
8 oz / 230 g jerusalem artichokes
1 pt / 570 ml vegetable stock
1 bay leaf
2 cloves

1 blade of mace or piece of nutmeg
1 tsp cornflour
1 tbsp water
¾ pt / 430 ml thick Greek yoghurt
4 oz / 110 g cheese, grated
2 oz / 60 g ground hazelnuts
2 oz / 60 g chopped mixed nuts
2 oz / 60 g fresh breadcrumbs

Peel and slice all the vegetables. Bring the stock, bay leaf, and spices to the boil, and cook the vegetables in it for 8–10 minutes, adding more boiling water, if necessary. Meanwhile, mix the cornflour and water and stir it into the yoghurt. Bring to the boil and simmer for 5–8 minutes, thus stabilizing the yoghurt. Remove from the heat. Transfer the vegetables to a lightly oiled or buttered baking dish. Boil the stock to reduce to about ¼ pt / 140 ml, removing the spices and bay leaf first. Stir in the yoghurt, and cook for 2–3 minutes before pouring it over the vegetables. Mix the cheese, nuts and breadcrumbs, and scatter over the top. Bake in a preheated oven at 180°C / 350°F / Mark 4 for 20 minutes or so.

Ratatouille

Serves 10

Vegetables brought to a plump, sweet ripeness by the hot, late-summer sun are some of the best partners for olive oil, and the Provençal dish of ratatouille *demonstrates this perfectly. Most cooks agree that a ratatouille should include onions, garlic, aubergine and sweet peppers, but here the certainty ends. Some leave out tomatoes; others leave out courgettes. Paul Bocuse leaves out peppers, and inexplicably includes carrots. I prefer to use all the Mediterranean vegetables.*

As this is such a time-consuming dish to make, I have given quantities for 10 servings. It is a good idea to make this amount, even if you are serving fewer people. Any left over will keep well in the refrigerator for several days, if covered. It could then be reheated and served as a side dish, or used in the crumble recipe opposite.

1½ lb / 680 g aubergines
1½ lb / 680 g onions, peeled and sliced
6 garlic cloves, peeled and crushed
½ pt / 280 ml olive oil
1 lb / 455 g green and red peppers, peeled
1½ lb / 680 g courgettes, sliced

2½ lb / 1.10 kg firm, ripe tomatoes, peeled, deseeded and chopped
1 bay leaf
sprig of thyme
3 parsley stalks
salt
freshly ground black pepper
3–4 tbsp extra virgin olive oil

Do not peel the aubergines, but slice them thinly and put them in a colander. Sprinkle with salt, and let them drain for 30–40 minutes. Meanwhile, cook the onions and garlic in 2–3 tablespoons oil in a frying pan until the onion is soft and translucent. Transfer to a large flameproof casserole and set over the lowest possible heat, using a heat diffusing mat if necessary. Halve the peppers, remove the seeds, and cut the flesh into thin strips. Add a little more oil to the frying pan, and gently cook the peppers, stirring from time to time, without letting them brown, for about 20 minutes. Using a slotted spoon, transfer them to the casserole. Rinse the aubergine slices, and dry them thoroughly by pressing them between pieces of kitchen paper. Add rather more oil to the frying pan this time, and heat it so that the aubergine slices sizzle and seal as soon as they are put in the pan. If the oil is not hot enough, the aubergine will absorb it like blotting paper, but once the slices are sealed you can turn down the heat and allow them to cook for 5–10 minutes. Again using a slotted spoon, transfer the aubergine to the casserole.

Cook the courgettes in more olive oil in the frying pan for 5–10 minutes, and transfer to the casserole. Add the tomatoes to the frying pan with the herbs, and cook for 15 minutes or so, until a good thick sauce is produced. Pour it over the vegetables in the casserole. The tomato sauce will seep down through all the layers of vegetables. Set the casserole over a slightly higher heat now, add a little more oil, if necessary, and cook, uncovered, for about 10 minutes. Add salt and pepper to taste, and stir in the extra virgin olive oil before serving. The *ratatouille* is delicious hot, warm or cold.

Variation ∞ A slightly quicker but less authentic method of preparing this dish, is to cook all the vegetables together, adding them one after the other to the same pan. Start by cooking the onions and garlic a little, then add the aubergine slices with a little more oil and cook for a few more minutes, then add the chopped tomatoes and strips of pepper, and finally add the courgettes, the whole cooking eventually to a meld of rich flavours with a soft consistency.

Ratatouille Crumble

Serves 4–6

5 oz / 140 g plain flour
1 heaped tbsp finely chopped
   parsley
1 oz / 30 g ground almonds or
   hazelnuts
2 oz / 60 g butter, diced

2 oz / 60 g Parmesan cheese, freshly
   grated
good pinch of nutmeg
1½ lb / 680 g *ratatouille* (see page 102)
3 oz / 85 g mozzarella cheese

Sift the flour, parsley and nuts together. Add the butter, and rub it in lightly and loosely until the mixture resembles irregular breadcrumbs. Stir in the Parmesan and nutmeg. Oil or grease a baking dish, and spoon in the *ratatouille*. Slice the mozzarella, and lay the pieces on top of the vegetables. Spoon the crumble topping evenly on the cheese, and bake in a preheated oven at 190°C / 375°F / Mark 5 for 20–25 minutes. Serve hot, while the mozzarella is still soft and melting; it becomes rubbery as it cools.

Vegetable Couscous

Serves 6–8

1 onion, peeled and chopped
3–4 garlic cloves, peeled and
  crushed
1 tbsp cumin seeds
½ tbsp ground coriander
1 tsp ground cardamom
1 tsp freshly ground black pepper
4 cloves
2 tbsp olive oil
1 medium aubergine, diced
2–3 courgettes, sliced

12 oz / 340 g ripe tomatoes, skinned and
  chopped
2 small turnips, peeled and diced
1 green or red pepper, deseeded and
  sliced
2 carrots, peeled and sliced
½ pt / 280 ml water or stock
8 oz / 230 g couscous
12 oz / 340 g cooked chick peas
2 tbsp chopped coriander
salt, to taste

Fry the onion, garlic and spices in the olive oil in a large saucepan for 2–3 minutes, and then add the remaining vegetables together with the water or stock. Bring to the boil, and simmer until the vegetables are tender but not mushy. Meanwhile, put the couscous in a colander or sieve, place over the simmering vegetables, and steam for 20–30 minutes.

Just before serving, stir the chick peas and coriander into the vegetable stew, bring back to the boil, and season to taste. Heap the steamed couscous on to a warmed serving platter, spoon the hot stew over it, and serve immediately with harissa or hot sauce handed separately for each person to take as they wish. If you cannot obtain harissa, you can make an equivalent hot sauce yourself.

Hot sauce
2 tbsp tomato or vegetable purée
1 tbsp olive oil
2 tbsp lemon juice

½ tsp ground coriander
¼ tsp cayenne pepper or chilli powder
2 garlic cloves, peeled and crushed

Mix all the ingredients together thoroughly, and let this stand for 20 minutes or so to let the flavours develop before using. A much more authentic and powerful hot sauce can be made by pounding fresh, hot red chillies to a paste, and mixing it with the other ingredients.

Asparagus Terrine

Serves 4–6

This is good eaten hot or cold, but is best of all just warm. Serve it alone or with a homemade tomato or watercress sauce. A hollandaise sauce would be delicious, but very rich, as would a garlicky mayonnaise.

Pancakes
2 oz / 60 g plain flour
1 egg
¼ pt / 140 ml milk
oil for frying

Filling
12–18 stems of asparagus
(depending on thickness),
trimmed to fit the loaf tin
lengthways

4 oz / 110 g tomatoes, peeled,
deseeded and diced
2 eggs
¼ pt / 140 ml milk *or* 3 tbsp thick
yoghurt and 2 tbsp water
1 tbsp finely chopped parsley
salt
freshly ground black pepper

Beat all the pancake ingredients, except the oil, together to make a smooth batter, and use it to make four large thin pancakes. Use three of them to line a well-oiled 1 lb / 455 g loaf tin, keeping one to cover the filling.

Wash the asparagus and boil rapidly in salted water for 3 minutes. Drain and refresh under cold running water. Scatter half the tomato dice over the bottom of the lined loaf tin and then put in the asparagus stems lengthways. Spread the rest of the tomato dice on top. Beat the eggs with the milk or the yoghurt and water, stir in the parsley, and season lightly. Pour this mixture over the vegetables.

Fold the overhanging pancakes over the filling, and cut the last pancake to fit neatly on top. Cover with oiled foil, and bake in a bain-marie in a preheated oven at 170°C / 325°F / Mark 3 for 50–60 minutes, testing with a knife point to see if it is cooked through. When it is done, the knife point will come out clean. Let the loaf cool slightly in the tin, then turn out, and leave to rest for an hour before slicing and serving.

Variation ∽ Replace the asparagus filling with a mushroom filling. Use wild mushrooms if available. Slice 1 lb / 455 g mushrooms, and fry with a little chopped onion or leek in olive oil until slightly softened. Use this mixture instead of the cooked asparagus stems when filling the terrine. This is very good with a fresh tomato sauce or a warm vinaigrette.

Aubergine and Red Pepper Terrine

*A fresh tomato sauce or a spicy tomato and onion salad is very good
with this, as is a bowl of warm couscous salad, flavoured with chopped
fresh coriander and mint leaves, spring onions, tomatoes and olives
(see page 68).*

6 Swiss chard or large spinach
  leaves, stems removed
3–4 large aubergines, trimmed
juice of 1 lemon
salt

freshly ground black pepper
extra virgin olive oil
3–4 large red peppers
2 oz / 60 g parsley, finely chopped

Blanch the spinach or chard leaves in boiling salted water for 3–4 minutes.
Drain, rinse in cold water, and pat the leaves dry. Slice the aubergines lengthways,
about ¼ in / 0.5 cm thick. Brush each slice all over with lemon juice to prevent it
discolouring, season lightly with salt and pepper, and brush all over with olive oil.
Place the slices on an oiled baking sheet, and bake at the top of a preheated oven at
200°C / 400°F / Mark 6 for 15–20 minutes or until the aubergine is soft.
Meanwhile, quarter the peppers, remove the stem, pith and seeds, and place, skin-
side up, on an oiled baking sheet. Bake for 10–15 minutes in the top of the oven,
moving the aubergines to a lower shelf. The skin on the peppers will blister and
can easily be stripped off. To assemble the terrine, brush a 2 lb / 900 g loaf tin with
olive oil, and place a long strip of foil down it lengthways to help turn out the
terrine. Line the tin with the spinach or chard leaves, keeping one back to cover
the terrine. Line the sides and bottom with slices of aubergine, and sprinkle on
some parsley. Build up layers of red pepper and aubergine, scattering parsley
between them and seasoning lightly, and finish with a layer of aubergine. Top with
the remaining spinach or chard leaf, cover with foil or cling film, and weight it
down with cans. Refrigerate overnight to let the flavours blend. Turn it out, slice,
and bring back to room temperature before serving.

Black Mushroom Roulade

Caroline Yates, one of the senior staff at Leith's School of Food and Wine, produced this when I joined the principals and teachers there for lunch one day. She used very mature mushrooms, almost black, which resulted in a stunning combination of dark roulade filled with a white cream. It makes an excellent main course, and can be prepared several hours in advance.

2 oz / 60 g unsalted butter	salt
1 oz / 30 g plain flour	freshly ground black pepper
2–3 shallots, peeled and finely chopped	4 eggs, separated
	3 oz / 85 g cream cheese
2 lb / 900 g mushrooms, roughly chopped or sliced	¼ pt / 140 ml double cream
	3 oz / 85 g pinenuts, toasted

Line a shallow rectangular Swiss roll tin with buttered baking parchment, and flour it lightly. Make a roux with half the butter and the flour, and put it to one side. In a very large frying pan, sweat the shallots in the remaining butter, and then add the mushrooms. Cook them thoroughly on a fairly high heat to extract as much of their moisture as possible. Cool slightly and put in a food processor with the roux, a little seasoning and the egg yolks. Process until smooth. Whisk the egg whites until stiff, and gently fold them into the mushroom mixture. Turn this into the prepared baking tin, smooth over, and bake in the top half of a preheated oven at 180°C / 350°F / Mark 4 for 12–15 minutes. When cooked, the sponge will feel springy to the touch and will shrink slightly from the sides of the tin. Lay a sheet of greaseproof paper on a worktop, and turn the sponge out on to it. Carefully peel off the baking parchment, and replace with a fresh sheet of greaseproof paper. Loosely roll the sponge between the two sheets of greaseproof paper while still warm. This will keep it pliable and will stop it sticking together.

Soften the cream cheese, and whip the double cream. Fold together, and at the same time fold in the toasted pinenuts. Unroll the sponge when cool, spread the cream on it, and reroll. Cover and refrigerate until required. Slice and serve.

Tomato Tart

Serves 6–8

A bread-making session led to this recipe. I had dough left over, and used it to make a tart case. I also had sweet, ripe tomatoes, some new season's garlic and extra virgin olive oil. Together they made an exquisite dish.

6 oz / 170 g white bread dough
  (see page 152)
2–3 tbsp extra virgin olive oil
12 oz / 340 g firm, ripe tomatoes,
  sliced
2–3 garlic cloves, peeled and thinly
  sliced

½ tsp sea salt
freshly ground black pepper
shredded basil or finely chopped
  parsley, to garnish

Lightly grease and flour a large baking sheet. Roll out the bread dough to form as wide a circle as you can without tearing it, and, of course, not bigger than the baking sheet. Carefully transfer the dough base to the baking sheet. Pinch up the edges all round to hold the filling in. Liberally brush olive oil over the base and sides. Arrange the tomato slices, slightly overlapping and interspersed with slices of garlic, on the base. Sprinkle with salt and pepper, and bake the tart in the top half of a preheated oven at 180°C / 350°F / Mark 4 for 20–25 minutes. Serve hot or warm, with basil or parsley sprinkled over.

Variations ∽ Instead of tomatoes, you could use aubergines, red peppers or courgettes. You should blanch the aubergines and courgettes after slicing them, and, if you can bear it, peel the peppers. For a really spectacular dish, you could make a single tart using all four vegetables.

A tomato tart can also be made using shortcrust pastry instead of bread dough. Use the pastry to line a 10 in / 25.5 cm flan ring or quiche dish, and bake blind for 5–10 minutes before brushing with olive oil and filling with garlic and tomatoes. Bake for 15–20 minutes only.

Tomato Puddings

This is one of my favourite recipes for high summer, when tomatoes are most likely to be at their sweetest. I first read a description of it in Jennifer Paterson's food column in The Spectator. *It has evolved since then. Unlike summer pudding, the filling should not be cooked.*

3 lb / 1.35 kg ripe tomatoes
sea salt
freshly ground black pepper
extra virgin olive oil

sherry vinegar
12–15 slices firm white bread, crusts
  removed
herbs, to garnish

Peel the tomatoes, and cut them in half. Scoop out the seeds, juice and pulp and put in a food processor with the skins. Process the pulp and skin mixture, then rub it through a sieve to extract maximum juice and flavour. Pour half the resulting liquid on to the chopped tomato flesh. Taste the mixture, and then add just enough salt and pepper to season and a generous splash of olive oil. Mix the remaining tomato liquid with a little sherry vinegar. Add salt and pepper to taste. Cut the bread into wedges, dip it into the juice, and use it to line 10 small moulds as if making individual summer puddings. Spoon in the chopped tomato flesh, and cover with a round of bread. Cover the puddings, weight them down, and refrigerate for 6–8 hours or overnight. To serve, turn out each pudding on to a chilled plate, garnish with herbs, and serve with more juice. A large tomato pudding can be made in the same way.

PASTA

Pumpkin Ravioli

Serves 2

Pasta
7 oz / 200 g strong plain white flour
2 eggs

You can make the dough very easily if you have a food processor. Put the flour into the bowl, add the eggs and process, in short bursts, for 30 seconds. The texture will be crumbly but soft. Scoop it all together, and form it into a ball. Let it rest, covered in cling film, in a cool place for 10–15 minutes. If you make the dough by hand, heap the flour on to a marble slab or your usual surface for making pastry. Make a well in the centre of the flour and slide in the eggs. Work into a dough with your fingertips, and form it into a ball. Let it rest, covered in cling film, in a cool place for 10–15 minutes.

Cut off a piece of dough the size of an egg, and roll it out as thinly as possible, ideally no thicker than ⅛ in / 0.2 cm. I find it easier to work with small pieces of dough, although accomplished pasta makers work with large quantities and still manage to roll it out thinly, using their hands to stretch the dough as they go. When you have a sheet of thin pasta, stamp out circles with a 2–4 in / 5–10 cm pastry cutter. The size is not particularly important; if you cut out large circles, you will probably only want two per serving, four or five if small. Repeat until you have used up all the pasta dough. Place the pasta rounds in a single layer, and not touching, on a board or tray covered with a clean tea-towel, and cover them with a barely damp tea-towel while you prepare the filling.

Filling

8 oz / 230 g cooked, drained
 pumpkin
2 oz / 60 g ricotta cheese, sieved
3 oz / 85 g ground almonds

1 tbsp *mostarda di frutta*, finely chopped
 (see note opposite)
freshly ground black pepper
freshly grated nutmeg

Blend all the ingredients together well.

Sauce
3–4 sage leaves
2 oz / 60 g unsalted butter, melted

Infuse the sage leaves in the butter over a low heat for 5–10 minutes, without burning the butter.

Ravioli

Place 1–2 teaspoons of the filling on to each pasta circle. Dampen the edges, fold over, and seal, to form half-moon shaped ravioli. Bring a large pan of water to the boil, salting it lightly or not, as you prefer. Add the ravioli and cook for 3–4 minutes until just tender. Drain, stir into the warm sauce, and serve with a grating of nutmeg and a sprinkling of Parmesan.

Variations ∾ Make the filling using 3 oz / 85 g crumbled or grated goat's cheese, 2 oz / 60 g ground hazelnuts, 2 peeled and crushed garlic cloves, a sprinkling of freshly ground black pepper and grated orange zest, and a tablespoon of finely chopped chives. Blend together well.

Instead of shaping the ravioli as above, leave the rolled out sheets of pasta dough whole, spoon out heaps of the filling at regular intervals on to half the sheets of dough. Place a second sheet on top. Press down around the edges and around the heaps of filling, and cut into filled squares or lozenges with a fluted pasta cutter.

Note: Mostarda di frutta or *Mostarda di Cremona,* as it is sometimes called, is a unique condiment from northern Italy, made by preserving fruits in a mustard syrup. A little apricot jam mixed with mustard proves a useful substitute. *Mostarda* is available in most Italian food shops and good delicatessens, but it is expensive.

Homemade Lemon Pasta

Serves 4

*Pasta is not difficult to make by hand. This is a good all-purpose
recipe. The lemon oil or zest can be omitted.*

10 oz / 280 g strong white flour	4 eggs
4 oz / 110 g fine semolina	2 tsp lemon oil *or* 1 tbsp finely grated lemon zest

Make the dough either by hand or in a food processor. For the first method,
heap up the dry ingredients on a work surface, and make a well in the centre. Slide
in the eggs and lemon oil or zest, and work in the flour gradually with your
fingertips until thoroughly mixed. Knead for about 10–15 minutes, working on a
floured board, to form a smooth, elastic dough. If using a food processor, simply
put all the ingredients in the bowl and process, in short bursts, for 30 seconds or
so. The texture will be crumbly but soft. Scoop it all together, and form it into a
ball. Cover the dough with cling film and let it rest in a cool place for 15 minutes.

Cut off a piece of dough about the size of an egg, and roll it out as thinly as
possible, about ⅛ in / 0.2 cm thick, on a lightly floured surface. Repeat this with
the rest of the dough. Let the rolled-out dough rest for 20 minutes before cutting
into the desired shape with a sharp knife. If using a pasta machine that rolls and
cuts, put the first rolled piece to one side while you roll out the rest of the pasta.
When you have finished rolling, the first piece of rolled pasta will be dry enough
for you to feed through the cutter. For *tagliatelle*, the rolled-out sheets of pasta
dough should be cut into ribbons about ¼ in / 0.5 cm wide. For *fettucine* or
tagliolini, they should be almost half that width, and for *pappardelle*, about ½ in /
1 cm wide. Hang up the strands of pasta as you make them, or loosely curl them
into nests. When ready, cook in plenty of boiling salted water for 3–5 minutes,
depending on thickness. When pasta is cooked, it should be *al dente*, that is tender
but still slightly firm to the bite. Serve with one of the simple sauces suggested on
pages 113–114.

For shaping pasta dough to make *ravioli*, see the recipe on page 110.

SIMPLE PASTA SAUCES

THE SIMPLEST way to make a sauce for freshly cooked pasta is to stir in uncooked ingredients, such as extra virgin olive oil, crushed garlic, chopped olives, tomatoes, crumbled or diced cheese and shredded fresh herbs. The heat of the pasta is sufficient to melt the cheese and heat through the other ingredients. Good combinations are extra virgin olive oil with crushed garlic, shredded basil leaves and chopped olives or tomatoes; olive oil, garlic and shredded chillies or sun-dried tomatoes; crumbled Gorgonzola and ricotta with diced mozzarella and grated Parmesan (a near classic *quattro formaggi*); shredded rocket leaves with olive oil and toasted pinenuts.

Celery and Sun-Dried Tomato Sauce

Gently fry a little finely chopped onion and garlic in extra virgin olive oil for a few minutes, until just beginning to turn golden brown, but without burning the garlic. Stir in a couple of handfuls of finely sliced celery and some strips of sun-dried tomato that have been soaked in hot water for 10–15 minutes. Pour on the soaking water, and simmer until all the liquid has been absorbed and the celery is cooked. Stir in some white wine and a little more olive oil, and cook for a few minutes more. *Fusilli* is a good pasta to serve with this sauce. Instead of Parmesan, crumble some goat's cheese on top.

Hazelnut Sauce

Put some shelled hazelnuts with a little hazelnut oil, some melted butter, a little crushed garlic and salt, freshly ground black pepper and freshly grated nutmeg, to taste, in a blender or food processor, and process until smooth. For a coarser texture, do not leave the motor on continuously, but switch it on in short bursts until the required texture is achieved. The more hazelnuts you add, the stiffer the sauce will be; the more butter and oil you add, the runnier the sauce will be. A similar sauce can be made with walnuts. Heat the sauce in a small saucepan before stirring it into freshly cooked pasta. Try it with *tagliatelle* or a short, chunky pasta, such as *penne* or *rigatoni*.

Herb Butter

Put equal quantities of chopped nuts and diced hard butter into a blender or food processor with a handful of chopped fresh herbs and a little salt and freshly ground pepper. Process until smooth and creamy. Blend this into freshly cooked pasta just before serving. It goes well with fine pastas, such as *linguine* and *tagliolini*, and will keep well in the refrigerator if covered. I think it is best not to use the more pungent, oily herbs, such as thyme, sage and rosemary, but you may feel otherwise. Fennel and almonds go well together, as do basil and pinenuts, coriander and walnuts, and chives and almonds. Experiment to suit your taste.

Herb and Gorgonzola Sauce

Tear up a handful of fresh herbs, and, using a pestle and mortar, pound them to a pale green paste with a couple of chopped spring onions and a little coarse sea salt. Stir this into freshly cooked fine pasta, such as *linguine* or *tagliolini*, and then stir in cubes of Gorgonzola cheese until the cheese melts. Serve immediately. Chervil, basil and lovage are good in this sauce, as are fennel, chives and marjoram.

Lemon Sauce

Infuse some pared lemon zest in butter over a low heat for 5–10 minutes, without the butter burning. Remove the zest, stir in some cream and grated lemon zest and cook gently until you have a well-flavoured cream. Stir in freshly ground white pepper and a little lemon juice to taste, and stir into freshly cooked pasta. Fresh pasta is best for this rich, creamy sauce. Try it with *tagliolini*.

Yellow Tomato Sauce

Sweat a little finely chopped onion, leek, carrot and celery in some extra virgin olive oil over a low heat, without browning, until soft. Add about a dozen roughly chopped yellow tomatoes, cover and cook until the tomatoes have collapsed. Add water from time to time if the mixture shows signs of sticking, but do not add too much or this will dilute the intense flavour. Rub through a sieve into a clean pan, reheat and season to taste. This is very good with freshly cooked *tagliatelle*.

PASTA DISHES

Spaghetti Genoese Style

Serves 4

1 lb / 455 g small new potatoes,
  scrubbed
1 lb / 455 g dried spaghetti
8 oz / 230 g slim green beans,
  topped and tailed

2 tbsp extra virgin olive oil
3–4 tbsp pesto
freshly grated Parmesan cheese

Bring a large saucepan of lightly salted water to the boil, put in the potatoes and boil for 7 minutes. Add the spaghetti and boil for 8 minutes, then add the beans, broken into pieces if you wish, and boil for 4–5 minutes. By this time, each ingredient should be perfectly cooked. Drain and put in a heated serving bowl containing the oil. Turn in the oil, and then add the pesto. Serve immediately, with the Parmesan sprinkled over.

Spaghetti with Uncooked Tomato Sauce

Serves 4

14 oz / 400 g dried spaghetti
4–8 sprigs of basil, or as many as
  you can spare
1 lb / 455 g firm ripe tomatoes,
  peeled, deseeded and diced

freshly ground black pepper
salt
2–3 tbsp extra virgin olive oil

This method for cooking dried pasta is one I learned from one of Italy's great pasta makers and experts, Eva Agnesi. It completely turns on its head the view that pasta should be cooked in fast boiling water. Bring a large pan of water to the boil, lightly salted if you wish, and put in the spaghetti, twisting and turning it so that it fits into the pan without breaking. Bring it back to the boil and boil briskly, uncovered, for 2 minutes. Turn off the heat, cover the pan with a tight-fitting lid and leave for 7–8 minutes. Meanwhile, pull the basil leaves off their stalks and shred them. Mix the tomato dice with the shredded basil, and season with pepper and salt. Drain the pasta (it will still be very hot), and pour it into a bowl containing the olive oil. Turn it until well coated, then fold in the tomato and basil mixture. Serve immediately.

Spaghetti alla Norcina

Serves 2

St Valentine was the martyred bishop of Terni. Terni is in Umbria, not far from Norcia, which is famous for its black truffles. Here the truffles are said to be at their best approaching carnival time, just before Lent, which makes them a fitting dish to serve for St Valentine's Day. I thought of this as I sat in a very ordinary restaurant not too far from Terni, eating a plate of Spaghetti alla Norcina. It was the only thing on the menu that tempted me, and such was the restaurant that I had no great expectations of the dish. It looked like spaghetti with a dark mushroom sauce, but when I ate a mouthful, there, amongst the mushroom, was the unmistakable chippiness of finely chopped truffle. Even a small amount of truffle will flavour and perfume a staple such as pasta to make it all taste of truffle. In the hope that someone might buy you a truffle for Valentine's Day, here is what to do with it.

2 oz / 60 g button mushrooms, wiped and finely chopped	1 truffle, scrubbed and chopped
1 shallot, peeled and finely chopped	8 oz / 230 g dried spaghetti
3 tbsp extra virgin olive oil	salt
	freshly ground black pepper

Fry the mushrooms and shallot in half the olive oil until soft. Stir in the truffle, and cook over a low heat for 8–10 minutes. Meanwhile, cook the spaghetti, according to the directions on the packet or according to the method on page 115, drain it, and toss in the remaining olive oil. Stir the sauce and pasta together, season lightly, and serve in heated bowls.

Tagliolini al Limone

(Pasta with Lemon Sauce)

Serves 4

Freshly made pasta is better for this recipe than dried pasta, as the sauce is light in texture and the flavour very delicate. Franco Verucci, sous chef at the Cavalieri Hilton in Rome, cooked it for us, and Emilio Licciardi, the maître d'hôtel, described to me in detail how to prepare it myself. Signor Verucci used tagliolini. Spaghettini *or angel hair can also be used. As with all pasta dishes, it is important to have the serving plates very hot. Shallow soup plates or deeper soup bowls are ideal.*

2 large lemons with good skins
2 oz / 60 g unsalted butter
3–4 fl oz / 85–110 ml single, double
  or whipping cream

white pepper
1 lb / 455 g fresh pasta

Peel off the zest of one lemon, and put it in a frying pan with the butter. Set over a low heat and leave to infuse for 5–10 minutes without the butter burning. Remove the zest. Add the cream, grate in the zest of the second lemon, and cook until you have a well-flavoured cream. Season with white pepper.

Cook the pasta in boiling water for 2–3 minutes, then drain it, but not too thoroughly, and mix with the sauce. Squeeze the juice from both lemons and add the juice of one to the pasta, adding more juice if required, to taste. Serve immediately.

This is a rich, creamy dish, despite the image of something tangy and astringent created by its name. If your pasta is particularly absorbent, you may well need to stir in as much as ¼ pt / 140 ml cream. Above all, the pasta should not be sticky in the sauce.

Vegetable Lasagne

Serves 6–8

The sauces can be made the day before required. If it is more convenient, the lasagne can be assembled 2–3 hours in advance and refrigerated until you are ready to bake it. It is worth making plenty of tomato sauce, as any surplus can be kept for another day.

Tomato Sauce
3–4 garlic cloves *(optional)*
1 onion
2 carrots
2 celery stalks
1 leek (white part only)
2 oz / 60 g fennel
2–3 tbsp olive oil

2 large (2 lb / 900 g) cans plum
   tomatoes
2 bay leaves
2–3 parsley stalks
sprig of thyme
sprig of sage or rosemary
salt
freshly ground black pepper

Peel and chop the vegetables, and sweat in the olive oil until the onion is just beginning to colour. Add the tomatoes and herbs, and cook, uncovered, for 2–3 hours on a very low heat. Allow to cool slightly before blending in a food processor or blender, or simply rubbing through a sieve. Season to taste.

Béchamel Sauce
2 oz / 60 g butter
2 oz / 60 g plain flour
1½ pt / 850 ml boiling milk

salt
freshly ground white pepper
pinch of freshly grated nutmeg

Put the butter in a heavy saucepan, and melt it over a low heat. Stir in the flour until you have a smooth paste. Do not allow the flour to colour. Pour on a little of the milk, and stir until smooth, then gradually add the rest, stirring continuously to avoid any lumps forming. When smooth, season to taste with salt, pepper and nutmeg, and cook gently for 8–10 minutes, stirring from time to time. Cool, cover and refrigerate until required.

Lasagne
1 lb / 455 g aubergine, trimmed
1½ lb / 680 g baby courgettes,
   trimmed
12 oz / 340 g baby leeks, trimmed
1 lb / 455 g lasagne

3 tbsp olive oil
8 oz / 230 g mozzarella cheese, diced
8 oz / 230 g ricotta, crumbled
4 oz / 110 g Parmesan or other hard
   cheese, freshly grated

Cut the aubergine into ¼ in / 0.5 cm slices. Bring a large saucepan of water to the boil, lightly salted or not, as you prefer, and put in the aubergine slices. After 2–3 minutes, put in the courgettes and leeks and boil for a further 2 minutes. Lift out the vegetables with a slotted spoon, put them in a colander, and refresh under cold running water to stop them cooking any further. Put to dry on layers of kitchen paper. Cook the lasagne sheets according to the directions on the packet, a few sheets at a time, if necessary, in the same saucepan of water in which you cooked the vegetables. If using freshly made lasagne that is still soft and supple, cook for 2 minutes only. Lay the cooked lasagne sheets on a clean tea-towel.

Liberally oil a square or rectangular ovenproof dish, and spread some béchamel sauce on the bottom. Cover with a layer of lasagne sheets, then a layer of vegetables, then some mozzarella and ricotta, and some tomato sauce. Spoon on another layer of béchamel, top with another of lasagne, and so on, finishing with sheets of lasagne topped with the remaining béchamel sauce. Sprinkle with the grated Parmesan, and bake in a preheated oven at 180°C / 350°F / Mark 4 for 50–60 minutes. Turn up the heat for the last 10 minutes, if necessary, to brown the top. Serve very hot.

Pasta with Broccoli, Chives and Blue Cheese

Serves 4–6

1 lb / 455 g dried pasta	4 oz / 110 g blue cheese, crumbled
12 oz / 340 g broccoli florets	1–2 tbsp chopped chives
3 tbsp cream or olive oil	freshly ground black pepper

Cook the pasta in plenty of boiling salted water according to packet directions. Five minutes before the end of cooking, add the broccoli florets. Drain together and toss in cream or olive oil. Stir in the cheese and chives and a little freshly ground black pepper. Serve immediately.

Rich Vegetable and Pasta Pie

Serves 6–8

*This is based on the rich pasta pies of Emilia-Romagna, which date
back to the Renaissance.*

Sweet Shortcrust Pastry
8 oz / 230 g plain flour
pinch of salt

2 oz / 60 g caster sugar
4 oz / 110 g unsalted butter, cubed
4 egg yolks

Mix the dry ingredients together, make a well in the centre and add the butter
and egg yolks. Gradually mix these in with your fingertips and gather the dough
together into a ball, trying not to handle it too much. Cover and chill for 1 hour.

Tomato Sauce
1 tbsp olive oil
1 medium onion, peeled and
    chopped
1 celery stalk, trimmed and finely
    sliced

two 14 oz / 395 g cans tomatoes
3–4 garlic cloves, peeled and chopped
¼ pt / 140 ml red wine
½ tsp dried thyme or oregano
salt
freshly ground black pepper

Heat the olive oil in a saucepan, and fry the onion and celery until translucent.
Add the tomatoes, with their juice, and garlic, the red wine and herbs. Cook on a
moderate heat until the vegetables are soft. Rub through a sieve and cook down
further if necessary until you have about 1 pt / 570 ml sauce. Season to taste, cool
and refrigerate until required.

Custard Sauce
¾ pt / 430 ml milk

1 tbsp caster sugar
3 egg yolks

Heat the milk and sugar together in a saucepan. Whisk the egg yolks in a bowl
and gradually stir in the hot milk. Strain the custard back into the saucepan, and
stir it continuously over a low heat with a wooden spoon until it thickens enough to
coat the back of the spoon, taking care not to curdle it by overheating. Pour it into
a bowl, and when cooled slightly, cover the surface with cling film to stop a skin
forming. Cool completely, then refrigerate until required.

Filling
1½ lb / 680 g dried pasta
olive oil
4 oz / 110 g mushrooms, sliced
4 oz / 110 g radicchio or chicory,
  shredded
4 oz / 110 g baby leeks, trimmed
  and cut into 1 in / 2.5 cm lengths
1 oz / 30 g butter

4 oz / 110 g blue cheese or goat's cheese
4 oz / 110 g mozzarella cheese
4 oz / 110 g Fontina, Edam, Gouda or
  Jarlsberg cheese
salt
freshly ground black pepper
2 tbsp finely chopped herbs
2 oz / 60 g Parmesan cheese, freshly
  grated

Cook the pasta in plenty of boiling water according to the directions on the packet. Drain it, and toss in a little olive oil to stop it sticking. Put to one side. Fry the vegetables in the butter for a few minutes until just wilted, and put them to one side. Cut the cheeses into small cubes. Use a large mixing bowl to assemble the filling. Put the cooked pasta in the bowl. If you have used long pasta, cut it into 2 in / 5 cm lengths. Stir in the vegetables, cheese and tomato sauce. Add the salt, pepper, herbs and Parmesan.

Pie
Roll out the pastry carefully, and line a deep, oiled cake tin with a removable base, leaving enough pastry to make a lid. Spoon in the filling, and heap it up to form a mound in the centre. Spread the custard sauce over it. Roll out the remaining pastry, and cover the pie, using the trimmings for decoration. Brush with an egg and milk glaze, and bake in the centre of a preheated oven at 190°C / 375°F / Mark 5 for 40 minutes. When cooked, carefully ease out of the tin, and transfer to a warm serving plate.

Fusilli Tricolore

Serves 4

If you can't get fusilli, *use another short chunky pasta shape that will hold a sauce well.*

4 tbsp extra virgin olive oil
8 oz / 230 g fine green beans,
  shelled broad beans or shelled
  fresh peas
8 oz / 230 g white button
  mushrooms

8 firm, ripe tomatoes
4 garlic cloves, peeled and crushed
¼ pt / 140 ml vegetable stock
1 lb / 455 g mixed green, white and
  orange *fusilli*
chopped herbs

First make the vegetable sauce. Heat the olive oil in a heavy-based saucepan or frying pan. Top and tail the beans, and snap them in three or four places, depending on length. Wipe and quarter or slice the mushrooms. Peel and deseed the tomatoes and cut the flesh into strips about ¼ in / 0.5 cm wide. Stir the beans or peas into the hot oil, and cook for 3–4 minutes, add the mushrooms and tomatoes, and cook for 2 more minutes. Stir in the garlic and the stock. Allow to bubble quite fiercely so that the stock and oil emulsify and the sauce thickens. Meanwhile, cook the *fusilli* in plenty of lightly salted boiling water according to the directions on the packet, usually a minute or so for fresh pasta and 8–10 minutes for dried. Drain the *fusilli*, sprinkle on a few drops of oil and stir in the vegetables. Serve in heated shallow soup plates, sprinkled with fresh herbs.

GNOCCHI

Potato Gnocchi

Serves 4

1 lb / 455 g cooked mashed potato
about 8 oz / 230 g plain flour

Mix the potato and flour until you have a kneadable dough. More or less flour may be required, depending on the amount of moisture in the potatoes. Knead the dough lightly for a few minutes, and allow it to rest, covered, for 30 minutes.

Put a large saucepan of salted water on to boil. Divide the dough into four, and roll out each piece, using your hands. Cut into cherry-sized pieces. Roll the pieces down the back of the prongs of a fork, and make a small indentation in the centre of each with your thumb. Drop a few gnocchi at a time into the pan of simmering water, and remove with a slotted spoon as soon as they rise to the surface.

These gnocchi are good tossed in melted butter or a fresh tomato sauce. You will need about 3½ oz / 100 g melted butter or ¼ pt / 140 ml tomato sauce for the quantity of gnocchi in this recipe. Hand round freshly grated Parmesan to sprinkle over the gnocchi.

RICE DISHES

Risotto

This is one of my favourite rice dishes. Nutritious, economical, versatile and easy to prepare, the soft, creamy texture of this northern Italian classic makes it the perfect comfort food. You will need a large, heavy saucepan, preferably with a rounded bottom to prevent the rice sticking at the corners, and a wooden spoon for stirring. The heat should be kept constant and moderate. If risotto cooks too quickly, the rice will be too soft and 'chalky', and if it cooks too slowly, it will have a sticky, glutinous texture. Keep the stock simmering, so that it is always hot when you add it, to avoid any temperature variations while cooking.

Basic Method

Heat butter or olive oil in the pan, and coat the rice well in it before adding any liquid. Then gradually add the simmering stock, about ¼ pt / 140 ml at a time, always allowing one batch of stock to be absorbed before adding the next. Stir constantly. Keep adding stock in this way until the rice is cooked. This should take about 20–25 minutes. You may find that the risotto is cooked to your taste before adding all the stock asked for in a recipe. The more liquid you add, the creamier the risotto will be, but the rice should remain just firm to the bite or *al dente*. If necessary, remove the pan from the heat, cover and allow to stand for a few minutes to absorb any liquid remaining in the pan. Season to taste, and serve immediately. Various flavourings and vegetables can be added during the cooking process, as in the following recipes.

Broccoli, Broad Bean and Mint Risotto

Serves 4

1 medium onion, peeled and finely
    chopped
1 tbsp extra virgin olive oil
10 oz / 280 g arborio rice
4 oz / 110 g small broccoli florets
2½ pt / 1.45 l simmering vegetable
    stock

4 oz / 110 g shelled broad beans
1 tbsp finely chopped parsley
8 mint leaves, finely shredded
salt
freshly ground black pepper
1 oz / 30 g unsalted butter
2 oz / 60 g Parmesan cheese, grated

Fry the onion in the olive oil in a large, heavy pan until soft and golden. Stir in the rice and broccoli, until well coated in the oil, then gradually add the simmering stock, as in the Basic Method opposite. Continue until you have used up about half the stock. Then, with the next batch of stock, add the broad beans and parsley. Continue adding more stock and cooking it to absorption until the rice is almost tender. Stir in the mint and seasoning, and cook in more stock until the rice is cooked to your taste. Stir in the butter and Parmesan cheese, and serve.

Risotto Nero al Balsamico
('Black' Risotto with Balsamic Vinegar)

Serves 4–6

3 oz / 85 g butter
1 small onion or shallot, peeled and
    chopped
1 bay leaf
small sprig of rosemary
10 oz / 280 g arborio rice

1 pt / 570 ml simmering vegetable stock
¾ pt / 430 ml simmering red wine
2½ oz / 70 g Parmesan cheese, freshly
    grated
balsamic vinegar, to serve

Melt half the butter in a heavy frying pan, and fry the onion or shallot until transparent. Add the herbs and rice, and when coated with butter, pour on a ladle or two of the simmering stock. Cook, stirring, until the stock has been absorbed, then add half the simmering wine. Cook, stirring, until this, too, has been absorbed, then add the remaining simmering wine. Continue cooking and adding stock, stirring fairly frequently, until the rice is cooked to your liking. Just before serving, stir in the remaining butter and the Parmesan cheese. Spoon into heated bowls and sprinkle with balsamic vinegar.

Pumpkin Risotto

Serves 4–6

12 oz / 340 g piece of pumpkin,
  deseeded and skinned
2 tbsp extra virgin olive oil
1–2 shallots *or* 1 small onion, peeled
  and chopped

12 oz / 340 g arborio rice
2 pt / 1.15 l simmering vegetable stock
1 oz / 30 g unsalted butter
2 oz / 60 g Parmesan cheese, freshly
  grated

Coarsely grate the pumpkin. Heat the oil in a large, heavy pan, and cook the shallots or onion until translucent. Stir in the pumpkin and the rice. When the rice and pumpkin are well coated in oil, gradually add the simmering stock, as in the Basic Method on page 124 until the rice is done to your liking. I prefer a very creamy risotto and tend to add more liquid than some might like. Stir in the butter and Parmesan just before serving in heated soup plates.

    Variation ✑ Instead of the pumpkin, use a mixture of grated carrot and very finely chopped celery. I once ate a risotto like this in Florence, and it was exquisite.

Mushroom and Red Wine Risotto

Serves 4

This is such a robust, powerful and unusual dish that, on the whole, I think it stands best on its own with perhaps a salad, cheese and fruit to follow for a simple lunch or supper. As to the wine that you use, I would suggest a cabernet sauvignon or a chianti, but I have the feeling that it is a dish which would lend itself to experiment. For mushrooms, use wild or cultivated, one single variety or a mixture. Shiitake, oyster and cup mushrooms are a fine combination.

3 oz / 85 g unsalted butter
1 onion *or* 3 shallots, peeled and
  thinly sliced
12 oz / 340 g mushrooms, cleaned
  and sliced
12 oz / 340 g arborio rice
½ pt / 280 ml red wine

2 pt / 1.15 l simmering vegetable stock
salt
freshly ground black pepper
2 oz / 60 g Parmesan cheese, freshly
  grated
parsley or chervil, to garnish *(optional)*

Melt half the butter in a large, heavy pan, and fry the onion or shallots until translucent. Add the mushrooms, and make sure they are well coated with butter before stirring in the rice. Bring the wine to the boil, and pour half of it over the rice. Cook, stirring, until it has been absorbed, then add the rest. Once all the wine has been absorbed, gradually add the simmering stock, as in the Basic Method on page 124. You may not need to use all the stock. The rice may be cooked to your taste after you have put in about 1¾ pt / 990 ml. Season and stir in the rest of the butter and the Parmesan cheese, and serve immediately in heated soup plates. Garnish with parsley or chervil if you wish.

Courgette and Herb Risotto

Serves 4

2 oz / 60 g unsalted butter
1 tbsp extra virgin olive oil
1 small onion, peeled and finely
  chopped
8 oz / 230 g courgettes, trimmed
  and coarsely grated or finely diced
2–3 tbsp chopped chervil, tarragon,
  basil or chives

12 oz / 340 g arborio rice
up to 2 pt / 1.15 l simmering vegetable
  stock
salt
freshly ground black pepper
freshly grated Parmesan cheese, to serve

Put half the butter and the olive oil in a deep heavy frying pan. Add the onion and cook gently until wilted, then add one third of the courgettes and herbs. Stir in the rice and, when glossy, add about ¼ pt / 140 ml simmering stock. Cook, stirring, until the liquid has been absorbed, then add a similar amount, and cook, stirring, until it, too, has been absorbed. Continue cooking and adding stock in this way, stirring fairly frequently to stop the rice sticking. When about half the stock has been added, stir in another batch of courgettes and herbs. I like to add them in three stages to keep a good colour and texture. Added all at once at the beginning, the greens cook to a dull khaki colour. The rice might be cooked before you have needed all the liquid. It depends on whether you like a drier or creamier risotto. Just before serving, season to taste, stir in the remaining butter, and scatter on some of the Parmesan, serving the rest separately.

Asparagus Risotto

Serves 4–6

This is a useful recipe for using up asparagus that is looking a bit 'tired'. It becomes something quite special when cooked with white wine.

8–12 oz / 230–340 g asparagus
1 pt / 570 ml water
1 pt / 570 ml good white wine (or use all water)

2 oz / 60 g butter
12 oz / 340 g arborio rice
2–3 oz / 60–85 g Parmesan cheese, freshly grated

Scrub the asparagus and break off the bottom third of each stalk. Bring the water and wine to the boil in a saucepan and cook the stalk ends until tender. Strain the liquid and discard the cooked asparagus. Return the liquid to the saucepan and boil the rest of the asparagus in the same liquid for 3–4 minutes, then remove with a slotted spoon and slice into ½ in / 1 cm lengths. Bring the cooking liquid back to a simmer. Melt half the butter in a frying pan and stir in the rice. Add about ¼ pt / 140 ml of the simmering liquid. Cook, stirring continuously, until the liquid is absorbed. Add more liquid and the rest of the asparagus, except the tips. Cook, stirring continuously, until the liquid is absorbed. Continue to add liquid and let it absorb until the rice is tender and creamy, but still just firm to the bite. (You may not need all the liquid.) Stir in the remaining butter, the asparagus tips and the cheese. Serve immediately.

GRAIN AND PULSE DISHES

Creamy Cep Polenta

Serves 4

Bradley Ogden is one of the best chefs in the San Francisco area. I love his food. This is based on one of his recipes.

¾ pt / 430 ml water
¾ pt / 430 ml vegetable stock
sprig of rosemary
8 oz / 230 g yellow polenta flour (cornmeal)
4 oz / 110 g unsalted butter
8 oz / 230 g fresh ceps, cleaned, trimmed and cut into ¼ in / 0.5 cm slices

2 garlic cloves, peeled and finely chopped
1 tbsp sea salt
1 tbsp freshly ground white pepper
3 tbsp finely chopped herbs, such as parsley, sage and marjoram
¼ pt / 140 ml soured cream

Preheat the oven to 180°C / 350°F / Mark 4. Bring the water and stock to a rolling boil in a large flameproof casserole. Add the rosemary and polenta flour, and cook for 5–10 minutes, stirring continuously with a wooden spoon to ensure there are no lumps. Cover and cook in the oven for 45 minutes, stirring from time to time. Remove from the oven, and add half the butter. Stand the casserole in a roasting tin full of hot water to keep warm. Melt the remaining butter in a frying pan, add the mushrooms, and fry them for 2 minutes. Add the garlic, and season with the salt and pepper. Cook for another 2–3 minutes until the mushrooms are soft. Add the mushrooms to the polenta with the herbs and the soured cream. Serve immediately.

Variation ∾ See also Grilled Polenta Slices with Mushrooms on page 42.

Dhal Tart with Cumin Pastry

Pastry
6 oz / 170 g plain flour
1 tsp ground cumin
pinch of salt
3 oz / 85 g butter or vegetable
   shortening
1 egg yolk, lightly beaten
iced water

Filling
12 oz / 340 g thick, cooked spicy dhal
   (see page 84)
1–2 tbsp chopped coriander, basil or
   mint
3 eggs, lightly beaten

To make the pastry, sift the flour, cumin and salt together, and then rub in the fat lightly until the mixture resembles breadcrumbs. Stir in the egg yolk and enough iced water to bind to a dough. Cover and allow to rest in a cool place for 30 minutes or so before rolling out and using to line a 10 in / 25.5 cm flan ring set on a baking sheet. Prick the base of the tart, cover with foil or greaseproof paper, add a layer of dried beans, and bake blind in a preheated oven at 180°C / 350°F / Mark 4 for 15 minutes. Remove from the oven, take out the paper and beans, and leave to cool.

To make the filling, mix all the ingredients together, having first seasoned the dhal with salt, pepper and any other spices you think it needs. Spoon the filling into the pastry case, and bake in the oven at 180°C / 350°F / Mark 4 for about 20 minutes, until just set.

Texas 'Caviar'

Serves 6

1 lb / 455 g dried black-eyed beans
bunch of spring onions
3–4 firm ripe tomatoes
2–3 garlic cloves
several sprigs fresh coriander

extra virgin olive oil
sherry vinegar or wine vinegar
coarse sea salt
freshly ground black pepper

Boil the beans for 10 minutes, drain, cover with boiling water, and leave for 2-3 hours. Final cooking should then take no more than 45–60 minutes, although if the beans are very old and hard, they might need longer. While the beans are cooking, prepare the rest of the ingredients. Trim, wash and slice the spring onions. Peel, deseed and dice the tomatoes, and peel and crush the garlic. Strip the coriander leaves from the stems and chop them; add the stems to the cooking beans, if you wish. When the beans are cooked, drain them and mix in oil, vinegar and seasoning to your taste. Stir in the rest of the ingredients and check the seasoning once more. Remember to discard the coriander stems before serving.

Quinoa and Lentil Strudel

Serves 4–6

Quinoa is a tiny, round, lens-shaped seed, originally from the Andes, but now cultivated in the United States and China. Highly nutritious and with a delicious flavour, it is an excellent addition to the repertoire of grain cookery.

2 oz / 60 g fresh breadcrumbs

2 oz / 60 g almonds, finely chopped

2 oz / 60 g butter

4 tbsp extra virgin olive oil

2 leeks (white parts only), trimmed and sliced

2–3 garlic cloves, peeled and crushed

4 oz / 110 g shiitake mushrooms, sliced

3 ripe tomatoes, peeled, deseeded and chopped

12 ripe black olives, pitted and chopped

2 tsp green peppercorns

finely chopped parsley

finely chopped basil, chervil or coriander

6 large sheets filo pastry

6 oz / 170 g quinoa, cooked and cooled

6 oz / 170 g green or Puy lentils, cooked and cooled

1 mozzarella cheese, diced

3 oz / 85 g pinenuts, toasted

Fry the breadcrumbs and almonds in half the butter and a spoonful of olive oil. Put to one side. In half the remaining olive oil, sweat the leeks until soft, and stir in the garlic and mushrooms. When the mushrooms are almost cooked, stir in the tomatoes, olives, peppercorns and herbs. Melt the remaining butter, and mix with the remaining olive oil. Brush the sheets of filo pastry with it, and layer them on top of each other, scattering a little almond and breadcrumb mixture between each layer. Leaving a 1 in / 2.5 cm border, spread the quinoa over the pastry, then the vegetable mixture, the lentils and finally the diced mozzarella and toasted pinenuts. Roll up and carefully transfer to a baking sheet. Alternatively, spoon the filling into a rectangular heap in the middle of the pastry, and fold it like a parcel. Brush all over with melted butter, and bake in a preheated oven at 200°C / 400°F / Mark 6 for 10 minutes, then turn down the heat to 180°C / 350°F / Mark 4 for a further 10–15 minutes.

EGG AND CHEESE DISHES

Cheese Fondue

Serves 4

*For fondues, there is no hard and fast rule about which cheese to use.
Many are suitable. Amongst the hard cheeses, Emmental and Gruyère
are the most commonly available. The semi-hard cheese Appenzell has
a rich, strong fruitiness which combines well with some of the milder
cheeses. Try Tilsit, the French Beaufort, the Norwegian Jarlsberg or
the Italian Fontina, either alone or in combination.*

1 garlic clove
¾–1¼ pt / 430–710 ml very dry
   white wine
1 tbsp arrowroot or potato flour
4 tbsp kirsch

1–1½ lb / 455–680 g hard or semi-hard
   cheese (see above), grated
freshly grated nutmeg
1–2 crusty loaves of bread, cut into
   1 in / 2.5 cm cubes

Cut the garlic clove in two, and rub the inside of a heavy saucepan or fondue pot
with the cut surface. Pour in the wine, and place over a gentle heat. Blend the
arrowroot or potato flour with the kirsch, and put to one side. As soon as there is a
fine, bubbly foam on the surface of the wine, but it is not yet boiling, start to stir in the
cheese, a little at a time. Stir constantly and do not allow the mixture to boil. When all
the cheese has been added and has blended in, stir in the kirsch and arrowroot
mixture, and continue to cook, stirring, until the fondue begins to thicken. Stir in
nutmeg, to taste, then quickly transfer the bubbling fondue, in the cooking pot, to a
spirit lamp on the dining-table. Spear the cubes of bread on long forks, and dip into
the hot, bubbling fondue before eating.

Variations ∾ There are, of course, many variations on the above. The Genevois
fondue might contain finely chopped dried morels, and that of the eastern cantons of
Switzerland may be made with dry cider instead of wine. I have come across a recipe
for pink fondue in which a dry rosé is used instead of white wine. Black truffles,
cayenne pepper, mustard, tarragon, peeled and chopped tomatoes and even curry
powder and diced pineapple are other published variations, none of them an
improvement on the original. The *fondue de l'armailli* is rather nice; in it the cubes of
bread speared on forks and dipped into the fondue are replaced by potatoes boiled in
their skins. Kirsch is not the only *eau de vie* used in the fondue; one based on pears
and plums might be used. If I made the fondue with cider instead of wine, I would
use Calvados as the spirit.

Glamorgan Sausages

Makes 12

10 oz / 280 g fresh breadcrumbs
8 oz / 230 g cheese, grated
1 leek *or* 4 spring onions, trimmed
 and finely chopped
1 tbsp chopped fresh chives
1 tbsp chopped fresh parsley
1 tsp mustard powder
salt

freshly ground black pepper
freshly grated nutmeg
2 eggs, separated, plus 1 egg white
milk, to bind
flour or breadcrumbs for coating
1 oz / 30 g butter
1 tbsp olive oil

Mix together the breadcrumbs, cheese, leek or onion, herbs and mustard powder. Season with salt, pepper and nutmeg. Mix a whole egg and an egg yolk into the mixture with enough milk to bind it together. Whisk the two egg whites to a froth on a plate, and put the coating flour or breadcrumbs on another. Divide the cheese mixture into twelve, and roll each piece on a floured board into a sausage shape. Roll in the egg white and then in the flour or breadcrumbs. Heat the butter and oil in a frying pan, add the sausages, and fry for about 10 minutes or until golden brown. Serve hot, warm or cold; they are good with homemade tomato sauce, chutney or pickle.

Courgette Flan

Serves 4

1 lb / 455 g courgettes
3 oz / 85 g Cheddar or other hard
 cheese, grated
3 eggs

½ pt / 280 ml milk
freshly grated nutmeg
freshly ground black pepper

Blanch the courgettes in boiling water for 5 minutes, then drain and thinly slice them. Grease a flan dish, and arrange the courgettes and cheese in it in alternate layers, finishing with a sprinkling of cheese. Beat the eggs and milk together, and add a little nutmeg and pepper. Pour into the dish and bake in a preheated oven at 180°C / 350°F / Mark 4 for 30 minutes. Serve warm.

Variation ⌒ Mix diced goat's cheese or grated Gruyère in with the grated Cheddar.

Farmhouse Cheese Pie

Serves 6–8

I developed this recipe as a means of tempering some Dutch farmhouse cheese that was very mature and almost too powerful in flavour to eat. It is a good way of using up odds and ends of cheeses. Alter the balance of grated cheese and cottage cheese if your main cheese is fairly mild.

12 oz / 340 g puff pastry	6 oz / 170 g plain cottage cheese
1 celery stalk, trimmed and finely chopped	6 oz / 170 g hard cheese, grated
	freshly ground black pepper
1 small onion, peeled and finely chopped	1–2 tbsp chopped herbs or watercress
½ oz / 15 g butter	beaten egg or milk, to seal and glaze

Divide the pastry in half, roll out each piece and cut it round a dinner plate (an octagonal plate makes a well-shaped pie). Place one piece of pastry on a greased and floured baking sheet. Gently cook the celery and onion in the butter for about 5 minutes, then mix with the cottage cheese and grated cheese. Add the pepper and herbs, and pile on to the pastry on the baking sheet. Spread the mixture to within ½ in / 1 cm of the edge of the pastry, and moisten the edge with beaten egg or milk. Give the remaining piece of pastry another roll or two so that it will cover the filling and meet the edges of the bottom piece of pastry. Press the edges together, and trim them with a sharp knife, making clean cuts without dragging the pastry. In this way you will get a well risen finish. Make several slits in the top to let steam escape, and brush with beaten egg or milk. Bake in the top half of a preheated oven at 190°C / 375°F / Mark 5 for 25–30 minutes, moving it to a lower shelf if it shows signs of overbrowning. Serve the pie warm.

Spanish Omelette

2 tbsp olive oil
1 small onion, peeled and thinly
  sliced
4 oz / 110 g cooked spinach,
  squeezed dry and chopped

4 oz / 110 g cooked potatoes, diced
8 eggs
salt
freshly ground black pepper

Heat the olive oil in a deep heavy frying pan, about 8–9 in / 20.5–23 cm in diameter, and fry the onion until golden brown. Add the spinach and potatoes, and distribute the vegetables evenly over the base of the pan. Lightly beat the eggs. Raise the heat under the pan, pour the eggs over the vegetables, and season lightly with salt and pepper. Draw the egg back from the edges as it sets, to allow the uncooked egg to run to the edges and cook through.

When the omelette is almost set all the way through, invert a large plate over the frying pan. Tip the frying pan upside down and allow the omelette to fall on to the plate, cooked side uppermost. Place the pan back on the heat, adding a little more oil, if necessary, and when hot, slide the omelette back in to cook the second side. When fully cooked, turn out on to a plate and allow it to cool. To serve, cut into wedges.

Variations ∽ Brown the diced potato with the onion, and instead of the spinach, use cooked asparagus, chopped into ½ in / 1 cm lengths.

Brown the diced potato with the onion, and while they are browning, sprinkle over a little turmeric, ground cumin, ground coriander and a few crushed cardamom pods. Substitute chopped watercress or rocket for the spinach. Season with a little cayenne pepper, as well as with salt and black pepper.

Desserts and Baking

The small selection of desserts and puddings which are included here make a good way with which to round off vegetarian meals, including fruit salads, baked fruit dishes, which are inexpensive and easy to make, and a number of puddings and pies.

The second half of this chapter concentrates on bread-making. For those people who would like to make their own bread but are put off by the mystique attached to it, you will find all the answers here, together with all the information needed to make good bread that will get better and better with practice and will help you to experiment. By changing proportions and ingredients, you will be able to produce a whole variety of different breads, carrying on the tradition of a cheap and nutritious food, which is also therapeutic to make.

Some popular bakes and biscuits end the chapter, from Teatime Scones (see page 158) and Pumpkin Seed Cookies (see page 159) to the more luxurious Biscotti di Vino (see page 161).

Fruit and Nut Casserole

Serves 6–8

1½ lb / 680 g dried fruit, such as
   apricots, prunes, figs, peaches,
   pears and apples
4 pt / 2.30 l hot Earl Grey or
   jasmine tea
piece of lemon grass
2 bay leaves

12 allspice berries
2 oz / 60 g pinenuts
2 oz / 60 g hazelnuts
2 oz / 60 g flaked almonds
2 oz / 60 g walnut pieces
3 tbsp sweet muscat wine *(optional)*

Put the dried fruit in a lidded flameproof casserole, and pour on the hot tea. Add the lemon grass, bay leaves and allspice. Bring to the boil, cover and cook in a preheated oven at 170°C / 325°F / Mark 3 for 1½–2 hours. Remove from the oven, and allow to cool. Toast the pinenuts, hazelnuts, almonds and walnuts in a heavy frying pan until just crisp and gold. When the fruit is just warm, stir in the nuts, and the wine if using. This is very good served with chilled thick Greek yoghurt.

Chilled Persimmon Creams

Serves 4

4 ripe persimmons with sound,
   unblemished skins
juice and grated zest of 1 small
   lemon

2 tbsp icing sugar
½ pt / 280 ml double cream

Cut a thin slice off the top of each persimmon to make a 'lid'. With a pointed spoon, carefully scoop out the pulp on to a plate. Make a purée of half of it in a blender together with the lemon juice and zest, and the icing sugar. Whisk the cream until firm, and blend in the persimmon purée. Roughly chop the rest of the fruit, and stir this into the cream. Divide the mixture among the fruit skins, replace the lids, and chill until required. The creams can, of course, also be served in wine glasses if the persimmon skins are not good enough to bring to the table.

Pear and Blackberry Crumble

Serves 4–6

*Crumbles are very easy, homely puddings to make, and they are very
popular indeed. The same dish is called a crisp, not a crumble, in
America. They are best served warm with chilled cream, crème fraîche
or thick yoghurt.*

4 oz / 110 g unsalted butter	3 tbsp unrefined sugar
1 lb / 455 g pears	6 oz / 170 g plain flour
juice of 1 lemon	4 oz / 110 g blackberries

Use a quarter of the butter to butter a pie dish. Peel, core and slice the pears.
Toss them in lemon juice to prevent them browning, and sprinkle with half the
sugar so that a good syrup is produced, and then put them in the pie dish. Dot
with another 1 oz / 30 g of the butter. Rub the remaining butter into the flour until
it resembles fine breadcrumbs. Stir in the remaining sugar. Mix the blackberries in
with the pears, and spoon the crumble mixture on top, pressing it down a little.
Bake in a preheated oven at 180°C / 350°F / Mark 4 for 30 minutes or so, until the
crumble topping is golden.

Variations ∾ These are almost limitless, but some of my favourite substitutes
for the pears and blackberries include gooseberries, plums and chopped hazelnuts,
cherries with chopped almonds and kirsch, pears and chopped crystallized ginger,
rhubarb and flaked almonds, blackcurrants and chopped mint leaves, and the very
unusual combination of bananas and mangos, flavoured with rum, with coconut
added to the crumble topping. Spices and chopped or ground nuts can be added to
the topping mixture of any crumble if you wish.

Winter Pudding

Serves 6

12 oz / 340 g mixed dried fruit
1 cinnamon stick
3 cloves
6 grinds fresh nutmeg
3 in / 7.5 cm strip of lemon peel
2 pt / 1.15 l Earl Grey or other
    fragrant tea

6–8 slices of wholemeal bread, crusts
    removed
thick Greek yoghurt or double cream
toasted hazelnuts or almonds

Cut the fruit into smaller pieces and remove any stones. Gently poach the fruit, spices and peel in the tea until the fruit is plumped up and tender. (If it is more convenient, soak the fruit in the tea overnight to cut down on cooking time.) Strain the fruit, discard the spices and peel, and reserve the cooking liquid.

Cut each slice of bread into two wedge-shaped pieces, dip them in the cooking juices, and use about two-thirds of the bread to line a pudding basin. Spoon the fruit into the lined basin, place the remaining bread on top to fit as a cover, and pour on more cooking juices to moisten the bread thoroughly. Cover with foil and weight down with a heavy object. Cool, then refrigerate overnight until required. When ready to serve, turn the pudding out on to a shallow dish. Pour on more juice if there are any dry patches, and then spread the pudding with yoghurt or pour cream over it before sprinkling toasted nuts over the surface.

Variation ⌒ For an early summer pudding, use white bread, and instead of the dried fruit mixture, fill the pudding with a delicious gooseberry and elderflower compote. Make this by cooking 2 lb / 900 g topped and tailed gooseberries with 1–2 heads of washed elderflowers in ½ pt / 280 ml water until the fruit is soft. Sweeten to taste, then sieve, letting the syrup trickle into a bowl. Use this to moisten the bread, and fill the pudding with the gooseberries and elderflower pulp.

Banana and Rum Tofu Ice Cream

Serves 4–6

If you like to eat puddings every day, it makes sense to look for low-fat and low-calorie alternatives to butter, cream and sugar. On balance, I prefer to eat puddings just occasionally and use the traditional ingredients rather than the 'ersatz'. Silken tofu is one of those derivatives of the useful soya bean. It is a pale, creamy substance with little flavour of its own and a texture like that of cream, but with only 2.6 per cent fat as against the 48 per cent of double cream.

4 ripe bananas
2 tbsp rum
2 tbsp honey (or more to taste)
juice of ½ lemon or 1 orange

1 packet silken tofu
pinch of ground cinnamon or grated nutmeg

Peel the bananas and put them in a blender with the rest of the ingredients. Blend until smooth, and then pour into an ice-cream maker, and freeze according to the manufacturer's instructions. Or pour into a container and freeze in a freezer or the freezing compartment of a refrigerator, in which case you will need to remove it after about an hour and beat it or blend it in a food processor until smooth and light, and then return it to the freezer for its final freezilg.

Quire of Orange Pancakes with Marmalade Sauce

Serves 6

8 oz / 230 g plain flour
¼ tsp salt
¼ tsp ground mace
3 eggs
12 fl oz / 340 ml milk

4 tbsp orange liqueur
1 tbsp orange flower water
4–6 oz / 110–170 g marmalade
whipped cream, thick yoghurt or crème fraîche

Sift together the flour, salt and mace, and make a well in the middle. Gradually beat in the eggs and milk, first to a smooth paste and then until you have a smooth batter. Stir in the liqueur and orange flower water. Let the batter stand for an hour before using. Use a non-stick or well-seasoned frying pan or a lightly oiled crêpe pan, and use the batter to prepare a stack of very thin pancakes, using the method given on page 56. If the pancakes are too thick, the finished dish will be stodgy. If you cover the stack with foil and leave it over a pan of hot water, you can prepare to this point before dinner or lunch, and leave the pancakes while you get on with the rest of the meal.

To serve, spread the top pancake of the stack with the marmalade, and transfer to a serving plate. Spread the next pancake with marmalade and place on top of the first. Continue until you have a new pile of pancakes layered with marmalade, cut it into wedges like a cake and hand the cream or yoghurt separately.

Variations ～ The orange and marmalade is but one version of this rather nice pudding. Jam, cream and icing sugar and honey, lemon juice and yoghurt are also good combinations.

The orange flavouring in the batter can be replaced with sherry, for example amontillado or oloroso, and the pile of pancakes served with cream whipped with sweet sherry.

Ginger Mousse with Lime and Honey Sauce

Serves 4

2½ oz / 70 g caster sugar
3 egg yolks
pinch of salt
½ oz / 15 g fresh root ginger,
  peeled and grated
6 fl oz / 170 ml double or
  whipping cream
2 limes

3½ fl oz / 100 ml clear honey
3½ fl oz / 100 ml water
¼ tsp cornflour

To decorate (optional)
2 fl oz / 60 ml double or
  whipping cream
4 slices candied ginger

Whisk the sugar, egg yolks, salt and ginger until thick and foamy. Whip the cream until firm, and fold into the mousse. Spoon into serving glasses and chill until required.

To make the sauce, squeeze the lime juice into a saucepan, add the honey and most of the water and bring to the boil. Blend the cornflour with the rest of the water, and then add it to the lime syrup. Stir and cook for a minute or two more. Chill and serve with the mousse which can first be decorated with cream and candied ginger.

Pineapple and Rum Soufflés

Serves 4–6

8 oz / 230 g peeled fresh pineapple
2 tbsp water
1 oz / 30 g butter
1 oz / 30 g plain flour
¼ pt / 140 ml skimmed milk
1 tbsp caster sugar
3 eggs, separated
icing sugar for dusting

Sauce
3 tbsp orange juice
1 tbsp caster sugar
1 tsp cornflour
1–2 tbsp water
3 tbsp rum

Generously butter individual soufflé dishes and dust the insides with sugar. Refrigerate until needed. Dice a third of the pineapple, and put to one side. Chop the rest, and put in a blender with the water. Blend for a few seconds, and then pour through a sieve over a bowl. Press out as much juice as possible, and then put the pulp from the sieve with the diced pineapple. Melt the butter in a saucepan, and stir in the flour. Cook the roux for a few minutes, then blend in equal parts of pineapple juice (using no more than half) and skimmed milk until you have a smooth sauce. Cook for a few minutes until it thickens. Remove from the heat, and stir in the sugar, the diced and pulped pineapple and the egg yolks. Mix thoroughly. Whisk the egg whites to firm peaks, and fold in carefully. Spoon the mixture into the prepared soufflé dishes, and place them in a roasting tin containing enough water to come a third of the way up the sides of the dishes. Bake in a preheated oven at 200°C / 400°F / Mark 6 for 12–15 minutes. Meanwhile, make the sauce. Put the orange juice and sugar in a saucepan. Blend the cornflour with the water and add to the saucepan with the remaining pineapple juice. Bring to the boil, and cook for a few minutes until thickened slightly. Stir in the rum just before serving the soufflés. Dust the soufflés with icing sugar, and, as you serve each one, break open the top with a spoon and pour in a little sauce which will cause the soufflé to rise in its dish.

Quick Banana and Cardamom Ice Cream

Serves 8

6 ripe bananas
juice of 1 lemon
¼ pt / 140 ml sugar syrup *or* 5 oz /
   140 g icing sugar, sifted

seeds of 10 cardamom pods
½ pt / 280 ml double cream
¼ pt / 140 ml single cream

Peel the bananas, and put in a blender with the rest of the ingredients. Blend until smooth, pour into an ice-cream maker, and freeze according to the manufacturer's instructions. Or pour into a container, and freeze in a freezer or the freezing compartment of a refrigerator, in which case you will need to remove it after about an hour, and beat it or blend it in a food processor until smooth and light, and then return it to the freezer for its final freezing.

Variations ⁓ For a quickly made peach ice cream, use 1 lb / 455 g peaches, peeled and sliced, instead of the banana, and orange or apple juice instead of the lemon juice, and omit the cardamom.

Replace the banana with 1 lb / 455 g cooked blackberries or blueberries or other available berries, and omit the lemon juice and cardamom.

For a quick marmalade ice cream, gently heat about 1 lb / 455 g marmalade until runny, strain it into a bowl, stir in the creams until well blended, and then freeze as above.

You can make quick ice creams using scented flower petals and buds. Scented petals from carnations or clove pinks, that have not been sprayed, petals from old-fashioned roses, and lavender buds can all be used. Make a syrup using water and sugar, stir in the petals or buds, bring back to the boil, and leave to steep overnight. The next day, strain the syrup, add lemon juice, blend with double cream, and freeze as above.

Muscat Grape Tart with Melted Butter Pastry

Serves 4

This is a very simple recipe which breaks all the rules about having a chilled work surface and cool hands to make pastry, and was given to me by Sheila Clark, a gifted, inventive cook who lives in Kent. If you choose large, ripe grapes, then it is not too much of a chore to peel and deseed them.

3 oz / 85 g butter
2 oz / 60 g sugar
grated zest of ½ lemon
6 oz / 170 g plain flour

7 oz / 200 g thick Greek yoghurt *or*
　6 tbsp whipped cream
1 lb / 455 g peeled, deseeded muscat
　grapes

Melt the butter gently in a saucepan. Add the sugar and let it melt and amalgamate but not cook. Remove from the heat, and stir in the lemon zest, then begin to work in the flour. The mixture will eventually become a stiff dough. Press it with your fingers or the back of a wooden spoon into a buttered baking dish, flan tin or 9 in / 23 cm flan ring on a baking sheet. Prick all over, and bake in a preheated oven at 200°C / 400°F / Mark 6 for 12–15 minutes, moving it to a lower shelf in your oven if it shows signs of burning.

When the base is cool and you are almost ready to serve the tart, spread the yoghurt or cream on the pastry and cover with the grapes. This is delicious served with a glass of chilled sweet muscat wine.

Tiramisu

8 oz / 230 g sponge fingers

¼ pt / 140 ml strong black coffee or espresso

3 tbsp cognac

8 oz / 230 g Mascarpone or cream cheese

4 tbsp thick yoghurt

4 oz / 110 g ricotta

3–4 oz / 85–110 g icing sugar

1 tsp pure vanilla essence

2–3 egg whites

1 tbsp grated plain chocolate

1 tsp finely ground coffee

Dip half the sponge fingers in the mixed coffee and cognac, and place in the bottom of a glass serving bowl. Blend the Mascarpone, yoghurt, ricotta, sugar and vanilla essence until smooth. Whisk the egg whites until stiff, and fold into the creamy mixture. Spoon half of it into the glass bowl. Cover with the remaining sponge fingers dipped in the coffee and cognac mixture, and then spoon on the rest of the cream, smoothing the surface. Sprinkle the surface with chocolate and coffee, and then cover and refrigerate for several hours before serving.

BASIC BREADS

Basic Ingredients

Yeast Bread-making is not a mechanical, unchanging process. Yeast is a living organism, and does indeed have a life of its own. All we can hope to do in making bread is to use its properties and get it to work for us. It grows and expands when conditions, such as temperature, moisture and food supply, are right. And the carbon dioxide gas caused in the expansion is what 'raises' the loaf to give it its characteristically spongy, airy, crumb texture. Fresh yeast can sometimes be bought from bakers where bread is made on the premises. Health and wholefood shops are another source of fresh yeast. Fast-action dried yeast, available from supermarkets, is simply mixed with the dry ingredients, and the dough is only required to rise once. It gives good results. I use fresh yeast if I can get it, or active dried yeast, also available from supermarkets. It comes in granule form, is mixed with water, and then added to the dough, which is given two risings. Some recipes specify active dried yeast. If a recipe calls for fresh yeast, you can replace it with about two-thirds the quantity of dried yeast. Approximately ½ oz fresh yeast or 2 teaspoons of active dried yeast are needed per pound of flour or 20 g active dried yeast are needed per kilo. A 7 g sachet of fast-action yeast will raise 750 g / 1 lb 10 oz strong flour.

Flour Gluten, produced from the protein in flour, is what gives bread the characteristic chewy texture. Strong wheat flour has the highest gluten content; rye flour also has gluten, but less. Other cereals, although containing protein, do not form gluten. Hard and rubbery, when flour and water is first mixed, the gluten becomes soft and elastic with kneading.

Other cereals can be used in bread-making, such as oatmeal and cornmeal, but not alone; they need to be mixed with a high proportion of wheat flour.

Strong flour, bread flour, unbleached strong flour, organic bread flour are some of the names under which you will find flour suitable for bread-making. It is useful also to look at the nutritional table on the packet. Strong flour will have a protein content of 11 to 13 per cent; plain flour, suitable for cake-making, will have around 9 per cent protein.

Salt Salt is used in bread-making to 'slow down', and thus control the action of yeast. It should be added at the rate of approximately 1½ teaspoons per pound of flour or 15 g per kilo.

Water The only other essential ingredient in bread-making is water, although liquid can be added in the form of milk, eggs, even cider, usually replacing a proportion of water. It is useful, when developing your own recipes, to remember, as a rule of thumb, that flour needs more than half its volume of water, that wholemeal flour absorbs even more water, and that on a humid day, you might need less water than on a dry day.

Terms and Techniques

Kneading Turning the heavy flour and water paste to a smooth, pliable, elastic, dough requires hard work, which is, nevertheless, quite manageable in small quantities. Domestic food processors can only mix, and do not perform the pummelling, stretching, tearing and gathering action which is kneading, although some electric mixers have dough hooks which perform something like a kneading action. It is a pleasure to feel the dough form under your hands, and unstick itself from your fingers as it becomes smooth and springy. On a floured worktop, hold the dough with one hand, and with the heel of your other hand, push the rest of the dough away from you. Give the dough a quarter or half turn, and repeat the process. Do this for 15 minutes, by which time all the dough will have had a thorough kneading.

Knocking back When the dough has had its first rising, all the air or gas is knocked out of it by turning it out on the table and thumping it around for a few minutes. It can also be given a further kneading, which will improve the quality of the baked product even further.

Proving This is the final rising of the dough once it has been shaped into loaves and put into prepared tins, moulds or on to trays. Proving should be done at the same temperature as the mixing and kneading, and the dough not allowed to form a hard skin. Covering with a damp muslin cloth is better than a tea-towel, which might hold down the loaf. Proving takes about 30 minutes in a warm room. Use this time to heat the oven so that the bread will go into a steady high heat at 240°C / 475°F / Mark 9. The tins are prepared by greasing and flouring.

Testing for 'doneness', the 'hollow' sound An undercooked loaf is still moist and heavy inside, without enough air trapped in it. When tapped on the bottom, it sounds soft and dull. When fully baked, light and airy inside, it will sound, when tapped, 'hollow'. A full tea caddy, when tapped, sounds different to the hollow ring of an empty tea caddy.

Optional additives Fat in the form of vegetable margarine or butter, in the proportion of 1 oz / 30 g to 1 lb / 455 g of flour, will give a slightly softer crumb. A proportion of water can be replaced by milk (whole, skimmed or semi-skimmed), which will also produce a softer, lighter crumb. Honey, malt, syrup or treacle in the proportion of ½ oz / 15 g to 1 lb / 455 g will sweeten the bread and provide extra nourishment for the yeast. It should be added to the warm liquid, not mixed or creamed directly with the yeast.

Flavours

This is where you can let your creative instincts take over. Remember only that substantial liquid additions should be calculated as part of the overall water content, and dry absorbent additions as part of the dry ingredients. Thus, if you use eggs or olive oil, you will need slightly less water; if you use a handful or two of oatmeal or cornmeal, use less flour. Some additions, such as powdered saffron or chopped, fresh herbs, for example, will not affect the proportions one way or another.

Cheese bread Add finely grated, hard cheese, about 3 oz / 85 g to 1 lb / 455 g flour.

Tomato bread Add softened, chopped dried tomatoes or tomato purée to the dough.

Onion bread Add finely chopped onion, fried to a golden brown; mix some into the dough, and scatter the rest on top before baking after glazing the bread with egg yolk beaten with milk.

Seed and herb bread When added to wholemeal or mixed meal dough, seeds give a chewy, flavoursome bread. The seeds can be toasted, or not, as you prefer. I like to use sesame, pumpkin and sunflower seeds. In late summer when your herbs go to seed, these too can be added to bread. Basil, fennel, dill, coriander, and parsley are all worth trying, as, of course, are the finely chopped leaves of the plants.

Olive bread Mix chopped, pitted green or black olives into the dough. Traditional olive breads tend to keep the olives whole and unpitted, but this can be dangerous if you bite into an olive hidden in a thick slice of bread. Chopped rosemary is a perfect partner to the olives.

Golden bread This is another idea to save for the summer when you can shred nasturtium flowers and leaves and chop the seeds to mix into the dough. This bread makes lovely cream cheese sandwiches, as does bread into which you have stirred marigold petals.

Orange bread Stir into an enriched dough (see Variations on page 152) 2–3 tablespoons of dried-up, last year's marmalade. This makes an excellent tea or breakfast bread.

Fruit and nut bread Into an enriched dough (see Variations on page 152), stir in chopped, dried fruit and nuts, for example dates and walnuts, stoned prunes and flaked almonds or apricots and hazelnuts.

Saffron bread Pounded or soaked saffron threads, added to an enriched white dough (see Variations on page 152), can be made into buns or a loaf.

Basic White Bread

Makes 1 large loaf

1 lb / 455 g strong white flour, at
   warm room temperature
1½ tsp salt

½ pt / 280 ml warm water
2 tsp active dried yeast

Sift the flour and salt together into a large warm bowl. Pour half the water into a small bowl, and sprinkle the yeast on top. After a few minutes, it will begin to become active and bubble on the surface. Make a well in the flour and pour in the yeasty liquid, and then the remaining warm water. With your hands, or a wooden spoon, mix the flour and liquid together until it forms a sticky mass. Turn it out on to a floured worktop, and knead for 15 minutes. Put the dough into a large, warm oiled bowl, and cover the top of the bowl, not touching the dough, with a clean, damp piece of muslin or a light tea-towel. Leave in a warm, draught-free place for about 40 minutes, after which time the dough will have more than doubled in volume. Knock it back, knead a little more, if you wish, and return it to the bowl to rest for 20 minutes. Turn it out on to a floured worktop, and quickly shape it to fit your tin or tray. You can be fairly heavy-handed at this stage, too, since no air should get rolled or folded into the dough. Cover again with a light, damp cloth, and leave to prove for 30 minutes. Bake in the centre of a preheated oven at 240°C / 475°F / Mark 9 for 15 minutes, then turn the oven down to 200°C / 400°F / Mark 6 for a further 15–20 minutes. Remove from the oven and turn out on to a wire rack to cool, but do not slice until cold.

Variations ∾ For enriched white bread, use 7 fl oz / 200 ml warm milk instead of the warm water. Sprinkle the yeast into half of it, and beat an egg and 2 oz / 60 g butter, melted, into the remainder before mixing it in.

For a sweet white loaf, mix in 2 tablespoons of honey.

To make flat olive oil bread, follow the recipe above until the dough has had its first rising, then knock it back, and put it on an oiled bake stone, set on a baking tray. (I have used a cast-iron griddle with satisfactory results.) Leave the dough, lightly covered with a damp cloth to rise for 20 minutes, then stretch it to fit the griddle or bake stone, and let it prove for 20–30 minutes more, covered. With your fingers, make hollows in the surface of the dough at regular intervals. Mix a little olive oil and warm water, brush it over the dough, sprinkle on coarse salt, and bake for 20 minutes or so in a preheated oven at 200°C / 400°F / Mark 6. Cool on a wire rack in the usual way.

Cider Bread

Makes 3 large loaves

*This is the method for making bread by hand using fresh yeast. Use
farm or unpasteurised cider if you can, which still has plenty of yeast
activity in it. Otherwise, choose a dry commercial cider.*

3¼ lb / 1.50 kg strong white flour
1 tbsp salt
1 oz / 30 g fresh yeast

1 tsp caster sugar or honey
1½ pt / 850 ml farm cider

Sift the flour and salt together into a large bowl, and make a well in the centre. Cream the yeast and sugar or honey together, and stir in a third of the cider. Pour into the well. Gather in enough of the flour to make a thin batter without breaking the flour 'wall'. Sprinkle some of the flour over the top, and let the yeast work for about 20 minutes until the batter breaks through the surface. Stir the yeast mixture into the flour, adding the rest of the cider until you have a workable mass of dough. Turn out on to a floured worktop and knead for 20–30 minutes. Put the bread into an oiled bowl, cover with a clean, damp cloth, oiled foil or oiled cling film, and leave to rise for a couple of hours in a warm place. (Alternatively, let it rise slowly in the refrigerator for up to 24 hours.)

Turn the dough out on to a floured worktop again, and give it a second kneading, but only for about 5 minutes this time. Shape into loaves, and put in oiled tins or on oiled baking sheets, cover once more, and let it rise for about 45 minutes. (With this dough, I like to use some for loaves, some for bread rolls and some for pizza bases which can be frozen at this stage.)

Bake the loaves in a preheated oven at 200°C / 400°F / Mark 6 for about 40 minutes. Turn out and cool on a wire rack before slicing.

Mixed Grain and Seed Bread

Makes 1 large loaf

8 oz / 230 g strong white flour	12 fl oz / 340 ml warm water
4 oz / 110 g wholemeal flour	2 tsp active dried yeast
1½ tsp salt	2 tbsp sunflower seeds
4 oz / 110 g medium oatmeal	2 tbsp pumpkin seeds

Sift the two flours and salt together. Mix the oatmeal with ¼ pt / 140 ml water, and let it stand. Sprinkle the yeast on to the remaining water, and let it stand for a few minutes. Make a well in the dry flours, and pour in the yeast mixture. Stir together, then add the wet oatmeal mixture and the seeds. Knead, and proceed as in the Basic White Bread recipe.

Grant Loaf

Makes 1 large loaf

For those who prefer the denser chewiness and the added nutritional value of bread made with wholemeal flour, there are many good recipes available. I like a loaf made with half or two-thirds white flour to appropriate proportions of wholemeal flour. But for a pure wholemeal loaf, probably one of the easiest and most reliable recipes is that for the Grant Loaf, developed by Doris Grant for her book Our Daily Bread. *It produces a soft, wet dough that you have to spoon into the loaf tin. It is not kneaded, nor does it have a second rising, and it is difficult to imagine that it will ever rise. It does a little. The secret is to warm all the ingredients and the loaf tin. Once used to the recipe and convinced that it will work, you can double the quantity. A food processor is ideal for this mixture.*

a good 14 oz / 400 g wholemeal flour	1 tsp sugar
1 heaped tsp salt	1 tsp active dried yeast
	12–13 fl oz / 340–370 ml hand-hot water

Mix the dry ingredients (except the yeast) using just half the sugar, and put them to warm. Mix the remaining sugar with the yeast, sprinkle it into ¼ pt / 140 ml of the hand-hot water, and let it work for 10–15 minutes. Meanwhile, grease a

2 lb / 900 g loaf tin, and put it to warm. Warm the food processor by filling the bowl with hot water or immersing it in a washing-up bowl of clean hot water. Once the yeast has frothed up, re-assemble the food processor, and put in the warm dry ingredients, the yeasty liquid and the remaining hot water. Process until you have a smooth but wet dough. Spoon it into the prepared loaf tin, and put the whole thing inside a large polythene bag. Leave to rise in a warm place for 25–30 minutes, by which time the dough should have risen to the top of the loaf tin. Bake in the middle of a preheated oven at 190°C / 375°F / Mark 5 for about 1 hour. Remove the bread from the oven, and turn it out on to a wire rack to cool.

Variation ⌒ You can replace the sugar with honey or black treacle for an even more distinctive loaf.

Oatmeal Soda Bread

Makes 1 loaf

These two quickly made breads do not contain any yeast. The raising agents are cream of tartar, bicarbonate of soda, and baking powder.

12 oz / 340 g strong white flour
2 oz / 60 g wholemeal flour
2 oz / 60 g medium oatflakes
2 tsp bicarbonate of soda
2 tsp cream of tartar

1 tsp salt
1 oz / 30 g butter
½ pt / 280 ml buttermilk (or milk
    soured with 1 tbsp lemon juice)

Sift the dry ingredients together into a bowl. Cut up the butter, and lightly rub it into the flour with your fingertips until the mixture resembles fine breadcrumbs. Make a well in the centre, pour in the buttermilk, and mix until you have a soft, pliable, but not sticky, dough. Add more liquid or flour as necessary. On a floured worktop, knead the dough lightly, and flatten it slightly into a circle, about 7–8 in / 18–20.5 cm across. Place it on a floured baking sheet, mark a deep cross in the centre, and bake for about 30 minutes in a preheated oven at 200°C / 400°F / Mark 6. Allow to cool slightly on a wire rack, but serve while still fresh and warm.

Cornbread

Makes 1 loaf or 6 muffins

4 oz / 110 g plain flour
4 oz / 110 g cornmeal or polenta
1 tsp salt
4 tsp baking powder

8 fl oz / 230 ml buttermilk
1 egg
2 tbsp groundnut (peanut) oil or melted
  butter

Sift the dry ingredients together into a bowl. In a separate bowl, thoroughly mix the buttermilk, egg and oil or butter. When you are ready to bake the cornbread, mix the wet and dry ingredients. Spoon the mixture into hot greased muffin tins or a shallow cake tin, and bake in the top half of a preheated oven at 230°C / 450°F / Mark 8 for 15 minutes if muffins, 20–25 minutes if in a cake tin. Remove from the oven, allow to cool slightly in the tin, then turn out on to a wire rack to cool slightly. Eat while still warm.

Quick Saffron Bread

Makes 1 large loaf or 8–10 rolls

few saffron threads
¼ pt / 140 ml boiling water
1½ lb / 680 g strong white flour
2 tsp salt

1 sachet (7 g) fast-action dried yeast
4 tbsp extra virgin olive oil
½ pt / 280 ml cold water

Put the saffron in a bowl, and pour on a little boiling water. In a bowl or food processor, mix the dry ingredients, and add all the liquids, including the oil and the saffron liquor. When it is thoroughly mixed, knead it for 10 minutes on a floured surface until smooth and elastic. Quickly shape it to fit your oiled loaf tin or baking sheet, or divide into 8–10 small pieces, shape these into rounds and place on an oiled baking sheet. Cover with a damp tea-towel, and leave to rise until doubled in volume. Bake in a preheated oven at 230°C / 450°F / Mark 8 for 35–40 minutes if a large loaf, or 15–20 minutes for rolls. Cool on a wire rack before using.

Boxty
(Potato Bread)

Makes 1 loaf

*Here baking powder is the raising agent, though, in fact, this bread
hardly rises at all, and is more like a potato cake.*

8 oz / 230 g potatoes, peeled
2½ fl oz / 70 ml water
8 oz / 230 g cooked potatoes,
   mashed
8 oz / 230 g plain flour

1 tbsp baking powder
3 oz / 85 g butter, melted
salt
freshly ground black pepper

Grate the peeled potatoes into a bowl containing the water. Stir with a fork, and then pour through a fine sieve into another bowl, pressing down well on the potatoes. Dry the grated potatoes on a clean tea-towel, and mix with the mashed potato. Let the potato starch in the water settle, and carefully pour off the water. Mix the starch with the potatoes and the rest of the ingredients. Shape the mixture into a ball and roll or pat it into a round, flat cake. Make a cross on top, dividing the loaf into four. Bake on a greased and floured baking sheet in a preheated oven at 180°C / 350°F / Mark 4 for 40–45 minutes. Serve hot, pulled into four pieces, split and spread with butter.

Potato Scones

Makes 12

1 lb / 455 g potatoes, peeled
pinch of salt

½ tsp baking powder
sifted flour, to mix

Boil the potatoes and when cooked, drain and mash them. Put on a floured worktop, and sprinkle on the salt and baking powder. Work in as much flour as needed to make into a fairly stiff dough. Roll out and cut into triangles or rounds, about ½ in / 1 cm thick. Lightly grease a heated griddle or flat, cast-iron frying pan, and cook the scones, turning them once. They should be quite doughy in the middle. Serve hot or warm, with butter, cream cheese or soured cream.

Variation ∞ If you use a large proportion of potato to flour, you can shape the dough into cakes, and shallow fry these in a mixture of butter and oil. These potato cakes are then very good served with freshly cooked asparagus and poached egg.

Teatime Scones

Makes 10–12

12 oz / 340 g self-raising flour
½ tsp salt
4 oz / 110 g butter
2 oz / 60 g caster sugar
1 whole egg, plus 1 egg yolk

3–4 fl oz / 85–110 ml buttermilk, plain
  yoghurt or soured cream thinned with
  milk
beaten egg and milk, to glaze (*optional*)

Sift together the flour and salt. Cut in the butter, and then lightly and quickly rub it into the flour with your fingertips until the mixture resembles breadcrumbs. Stir in the sugar. Beat the egg and egg yolk with about half the liquid, and stir into the dry ingredients, adding more liquid as necessary to form a dough. On a lightly floured board, gather the dough together, and knead briefly and lightly until it coheres. Roll out to about ¾ in / 2 cm thick and cut into 2 in / 5 cm rounds with a fluted pastry cutter. Place the scones on a greased and floured baking sheet, making sure that they are touching, brush with egg and milk, if using, and bake in a preheated oven at 200°C / 400°F / Mark 6 for 10–12 minutes.

Wholemeal Fruit and Nut Biscuits, American Style

Makes 18–24

These 'biscuits' are, essentially, what the British would call scones.

2 tsp active dried yeast
2 tbsp warm water
1¼ lb / 570 g self-raising wholemeal
  flour
1 oz / 30 g light muscovado sugar
½ tsp baking powder

4 oz / 110 g sunflower margarine or
  other vegetable shortening, plus extra
  for brushing
8 fl oz / 230 ml buttermilk
4 oz / 110 g chopped nuts
4 oz / 110 g dried fruit, chopped

Grease a roasting tin or baking sheet, and preheat the oven to 200°C / 400°F / Mark 6. Dissolve the yeast in the warm water. Mix the flour, sugar and baking powder together, and rub in the fat until the mixture forms lumps the size of hazelnuts. Mix the buttermilk and yeast mixture together, and add it to the dry mixture together with the nuts and fruit. Stir together with a fork until the dough just binds. Roll out to ½ in / 1 cm thick on a floured worktop. Cut out with a 2 in / 5 cm pastry cutter, and place close together in the roasting tin or on the baking sheet. Cover with a clean, damp cloth, and leave to prove for 1 hour. (The dough will rise but not double in volume.) Bake for 15–20 minutes, until golden brown. Brush the tops with melted margarine or butter, and serve hot or warm.

Pumpkin Seed Cookies

Makes about 24

American cookbooks are a good source of sweet pumpkin recipes – pies, puddings, meringues, soufflés and ice-creams, not to mention cookies. This one is based on a recipe from a book called The Joy of Cooking. *I have gradually changed almost every ingredient in it but still followed the same basic method.*

12 oz / 340 g golden syrup
4 oz / 110 g unsalted butter
generous 4½ oz / 125 g plain flour,
    sifted

½ tsp salt
3–4oz / 85–110 g toasted pumpkin seeds

In a small, heavy saucepan, boil the syrup and butter together for 30 seconds or so, and remove from the heat. Tip in half the flour and the salt, and beat vigorously until there are no lumps. Add the remaining flour, and beat the mixture until it is smooth and leaves the side of the pan. Stir in the pumpkin seeds. Drop heaped teaspoonfuls of the mixture on to two well-greased baking sheets. Bake in a preheated oven at 180°C / 350°F / Mark 4 for 12–15 minutes. The cookies will be soft when you transfer them to a rack but will firm up as they cool.

Variations ⮑ Golden syrup can be replaced with molasses, maple syrup or thick syrup made of muscovado sugar.

Replace the pumpkin seeds, a couple of tablespoons of flour and a little of the butter with peanut butter, smooth or crunchy, and peanut butter addicts will be your friends for life.

Use hazelnut or walnut oil in place of some of the butter, and some chopped hazelnuts or walnuts for very elegant biscuits.

Cantuccini
(Almond Dipping Biscuits)

Makes about 48

*When cooled completely, these hard biscuits, full of almonds,
keep very well in an airtight tin, so it is worth making them
in large quantities.*

1 lb / 455 g whole unblanched
  almonds
10 oz / 280 g golden granulated
  (unrefined) sugar
8 oz / 230 g plain flour
1 tsp ground cinnamon *(optional)*

2 tsp baking powder
3 tbsp melted butter
2 eggs, lightly beaten
1 egg yolk and 4 tbsp milk, beaten
  together, to glaze

Place the almonds in a shallow roasting tin and toast them in the oven. Grind a quarter of the almonds with a quarter of the sugar, and put into a large bowl. Stir in the flour, all the remaining sugar, the cinnamon, if using, and baking powder, and mix well. Coarsely chop half the remaining almonds and stir into the mixture with the remaining whole almonds. Add the melted butter and beaten eggs, and knead lightly until the dough is thoroughly combined. Divide the dough into four pieces and, with your hands, roll out each piece into a log. Flatten to about ¾ in / 2 cm thickness, then carefully transfer to a buttered and floured baking sheet. Brush with the glaze and bake in the top of a preheated oven at 190°C / 375°F / Mark 5 for 20–25 minutes until golden brown and a skewer inserted in the middle comes out clean. Cut into diagonal slices about ¾ in / 2 cm wide. Switch off the oven, and let the biscuits stand in the bottom of the oven for 15 minutes. Transfer the slices to a rack to cool even more. Allow them to get completely cold, and then store in an airtight container.

Biscotti di Vino

(Crisp Wine Biscuits)

Makes 10–12

*A food processor makes short work of this recipe; first mix the dry
ingredients and then add the liquid. It makes a rather soft, pasty
dough. And if you use red wine, the dough turns an alarming and
unappetizing blue-grey. This changes on baking to a nice warm brown.*

1 lb / 455 g plain flour
5 oz / 140 g caster sugar
1 tsp salt
1 tbsp baking powder
6 tbsp olive oil

6 tbsp muscat wine, port, sherry or
    full-bodied dry red table wine
3–4 oz / 85–110 g plain flour for
    kneading and rolling out

Sift the dry ingredients together into a bowl. Make a hollow in the centre, and
pour in the oil and wine. Mix thoroughly and knead lightly on a floured worktop
until smooth. Break off a walnut-sized piece of dough, and roll it into a rope about
4 in /10 cm long. Pinch the ends together to form a ring, and place on a greased
and floured baking sheet. Continue with the rest of the dough. Bake in the top half
of a preheated oven at 180°C / 350°F / Mark 4 for 20 minutes, and then for a
further 15–20 minutes towards the bottom of the oven at 150°C / 300°F / Mark 2.
Remove the biscuits and allow to cool on a wire rack. When completely cold, store
in an airtight container.

Variations ⁓ A variation on this recipe is to replace the wine with a water and
Pernod or Pastis mixture, brushing the biscuits with a sugar and water glaze after
the first baking and sprinkling on fennel or anise seeds.

If you prefer not to bake with olive oil, you can use melted butter.

Straccia Denti

(Very Hard Almond Biscuits)

Makes 4 dozen

1 lb / 455 g almonds
14 oz / 395 g honey
10 oz / 280 g plain flour

3 egg whites
a little butter

Blanch the almonds, remove the skins, and slice the nuts lengthways, or split them. Mix with the honey and flour, keeping back a tablespoon of the flour. Whisk the egg whites to stiff peaks, and fold into the almond mixture. Butter and flour baking sheets, and put spoonfuls of the mixture on to them, leaving space for it to spread. Bake in a preheated oven at 170°C / 325°F / Mark 3 until the biscuits are a pale gold. Let them cool on the baking sheets and then remove, and when completely cold, store in an airtight tin.

Entertaining

With a little forethought and planning, entertaining on a large or small scale need not be a daunting prospect. This chapter includes basic information and helpful advice plus short-cuts and time-savers that no one but you will notice, ending with some suggested menus for complete meals which you can stick to or adapt to suit your own style and taste.

Planning the meal

It is not a good idea to have hot courses exclusively, unless you have plenty of kitchen help to share the tasks. A cold first course, followed by a hot main course, vegetables or salad, then cheese and finally one cold or one hot dessert, is a workable format for the single-handed cook.

Advanced preparation

Avoid having to plate every course, especially hot ones. This is fine if there are two or three helpers, but can be a disaster otherwise.

Salad greens, such as lettuce, radicchio, endive, fennel and celery, can be trimmed and well washed, but any roots should be left on and everything put, roots down, in a large bowl of water, to which you should add ice cubes from time to time. Keep this in a cool place, and they will stay fresh for a day or two, although they will inevitably lose some vitamins.

If you peel, halve, deseed and thinly slice a cucumber, then salt and drain it for several hours, and finally rinse and squeeze dry in kitchen paper, it will keep, covered, in the refrigerator, for 2–3 days.

Most vegetables can be washed, trimmed or peeled, sliced and blanched, and put in airtight containers in the refrigerator several hours before they are needed. After blanching, put them in a bowl of ice-cold water, and then drain them. Again, loss of vitamins is the price to pay for convenience.

Most kinds of soups, hot or cold, can be made the day before, and the garnish, such as cream, sherry, croûtons or torn herbs, can be added at the last moment.

A tub of double cream or thick yogurt mixed with half the quantity of good jam, jelly or marmalade can be frozen for a very acceptable ice cream. Remember to leave enough time for any ice cream to thaw a little before serving. Good vanilla ice cream can be used as a base for toppings of honey, chestnut purée, crumbled cake, rum-soaked raisins or chopped crystallized fruits.

MENUS

Casual Supper

Hummus (see page 44)
Radishes with Three Butters (see page 44)
Cucumber and Mint Salad (see page 64)

Vegetable Couscous (see page 104)

Orange, Onion and Olive Salad (see page 63)
Chick Pea and Vegetable Salad (see page 69)

Pear and Blackberry Crumble (see page 140)

Summer Lunch

Carrot and Peach Soup (see page 24)

Aubergine and Red Pepper Terrine (see page 106)
Couscous Salad (see page 68)
Fresh Tomato Sauce

Banana and Rum Tofu Ice Cream (see page 142)

Winter Warmer

Black Bean Soup (see page 15)
or *Carciofi all Romana (see page 33)*

Winter Vegetable Gratin (see page 101)
or *Leek, Potato and Parmesan Strudel (see page 100)*
Glazed Chestnuts (see page 76)
Aligot (see page 82)

Winter Pudding (see page 141)

Supper Party

Spiced Carrot and Parsnip Soup (see page 14) with
Stir-fried Vegetables and Toasted Sesame Tartlets (see page 37)

Llapingachos (see page 40)
or *Aubergine and Red Pepper Terrine (see page 106)*

Pumpkin Ravioli (see page 110)
or *Vegetable Lasagne (see page 118)*
Green Salad

Pineapple and Rum Soufflés (see page 144)
or *Quire of Orange Pancakes with Marmalade Sauce (see page 142)*

Christmas Dinner

with the aperitifs:
Gougère (see page 38)

Pumpkin and Almond Soup (see page 17)

Rich Vegetable and Pasta Pie (see page 120)

Fennel and Pomegranate Salad (see page 61)

Chilled Persimmon Creams (see page 139)

Cantuccini (see page 160)
Biscotti di Vino (see page 161) and
Straccia Denti (see page 162) with
a rich sweet dessert wine

Italian Meal

Minestrone (see page 19)
or *Carciofi all Romana (see page 33)*

Vegetable Lasagne (see page 118)
Marinated Carrot Salad (see page 61) and
Radicchio and Parmesan Salad (see page 70)
or *Grilled Radicchio (see page 82)*

Tiramisu (see page 147)

Vegetarian Feast

Aubergine, Corn and Tomato Soup (see page 13)
or *Vegetable Gumbo (see page 20)* with
Spanakopitta (see page 39)

Tomato Tart (see page 108)
or *Vegetable and Tofu Creams* with
Tomato and Basil Vinaigrette (see page 29)

Black Mushroom Roulade (see page 107)
or *Celeriac, Pumpkin and Walnut Crumble (see page 94)*

Quinoa and Lentil Strudel (see page 131)
or *Creamy Cep Polenta (see page 129)*

Ginger Mousse with Lime and Honey Sauce (see page 143)
or *Quick Banana and Cardamom Ice Cream (see page 145)*
or *Muscat Grape Tart with Melted Butter Pastry (see page 146)*

Index

additives, bread-making, 150
advanced preparations, 164
aligot, 82-3
almonds:
asparagus and almond soup,
16
asparagus and almonds in
filo, 89
cantuccini, 160
pumpkin and almond soup,
17
straccia denti, 162
aloo gobi subji, 83
artichokes:
artichoke and asparagus
casserole in butter and
cider sauce, 28
artichoke and potato
casserole, 90-1
carciofi all Romana, 33
artichokes, Jerusalem *see*
Jerusalem artichokes
asparagus:
artichoke and asparagus
casserole in butter and
cider sauce, 28
asparagus and almond soup,
16
asparagus and almonds in
filo, 89
asparagus and potato
omelette, 47
asparagus risotto, 128
asparagus soup, 12-13

asparagus terrine, 105
cheese and asparagus
pastries, 41
salade Huguette, 67
aubergines:
aubergine and okra brown
curry, 95
aubergines and red pepper
terrine, 106
aubergine, corn and tomato
soup, 13
aubergine, okra and tomato
stew, 91
aubergine salad, 46
grilled aubergine, onion and
pepper salad with warm
garlic and pinenut cream,
72
ratatouille, 102-3
vegetable lasagne, 118-19
baking, 138, 148-62
balsamic vinegar:
risotto nero al balsamico, 125
bananas:
banana and rum tofu ice
cream, 142
quick banana and cardamom
ice cream, 145
barley:
wild greens and barley
'risotto', 98
basil, and tomato vinaigrette, 29
basmati rice, 85
batter pudding, Gruyère and

courgette, 51
bean sprouts:
eggs casho, 48
beans:
salad of peas and beans, 66
soaking and cooking, 7
*see also individual types of
bean*
béchamel sauce, 118
beetroot and tomato soup, 21
Bertolli, Paul, 14
biscuits:
biscotti di vino, 161
cantuccini, 160
pumpkin seed cookies, 159
straccia denti, 162
black bean soup, 15
black-eyed beans:
Texas 'caviar', 130-1
'black' risotto with balsamic
vinegar, 125
blackberries:
pear and blackberry crumble,
140
Bourdin, Michel, 54
boxty, 157
bread, 138, 148-57
basic white bread, 152
boxty, 157
bread and tomato salad, 71
cheese bread, 150
cider bread, 153
cornbread, 156
fruit and nut bread, 151

Glamorgan sausages, 133
golden bread, 151
Grant loaf, 154-5
grilled goat's cheese on
    country bread, 50
herb bread, 151
mixed grain and seed bread,
    154
oatmeal soda bread, 155
olive bread, 151
onion bread, 150
orange bread, 151
quick saffron bread, 156
saffron bread, 151
seed bread, 151
tomato bread, 150
tomato puddings, 109
winter pudding, 141
broad beans:
    broad beans and peas with
        cream and lettuce, 74
    broccoli, broad bean and
        mint risotto, 125
broccoli:
    broccoli, broad bean and
        mint risotto, 125
    broccoli with tomato and soy
        butter, 32
    pasta with broccoli,
        chives and blue cheese,
        119
broth, vegetable, 11
buckwheat galettes, 57
bulgar wheat, 86
butter, 6
    herb butter, 114
    melted butter pastry, 146
    radishes with three butters,
        44

tomato and soy, 32
buttermilk:
    cornbread, 156
    teatime scones, 158

cabbage:
    cabbage stuffed with wild
        mushrooms, 92
    coleslaw, 66-7
    sweet and sour cabbage, 73
    see also red cabbage
cantuccini, 160
carciofi all romana, 33
cardamom:
    quick banana and cardamom
        ice cream, 145
Carluccio, Antonio, 42
carrots:
    carrot and peach soup, 24
    lemon-glazed carrots, 74
    marinated carrot salad, 61
    spiced carrot and parsnip
        soup, 14
casseroles and stews:
    artichoke and potato
        casserole, 90-1
    aubergine, okra and tomato
        stew, 91
    fruit and nut casserole, 139
    see also curries
cauliflower:
    aloo gobi subji, 83
Cavalieri Hilton, Rome, 117
'caviar', Texas, 130-1
celeriac:
    celeriac, pumpkin and walnut
        crumble, 94
    celeriac with lime, 75
celery and sun-dried tomato

sauce, 113
cep polenta, creamy, 129
cheese, 6
    aligot, 82-3
    asparagus and almonds in
        filo, 89
    basic savoury soufflé, 54
    cheese and asparagus
        pastries, 41
    cheese bread, 150
    cheese fondue, 132
    cheese soufflés in paper cases,
        55
    courgette flan, 133
    farmhouse cheese pie, 134
    fennel with cheese sauce, 30-1
    fonduta, 50
    Glamorgan sausages, 133
    gougère, 38
    Gruyère and courgette batter
        pudding, 51
    herb and Gorgonzola sauce,
        114
    honey-glazed Stilton
        potatoes, 90
    leek, potato and Parmesan
        strudel, 100
    llapingachos, 40
    onion and cheese soup under
        a soufflé, 22-3
    pasta with broccoli, chives
        and blue cheese, 119
    potted cheese, 31
    radicchio and Parmesan
        salad, 70
    rich vegetable and pasta pie,
        120-1
    roasted garlic, Gorgonzola
        and toasted pinenuts, 43

Roquefort profiteroles, 52
  Stilton mousse, 34
  traditional baked rarebit, 52
  wild greens and wild rice
    crumble, 99
  winter vegetable gratin, 101
cheese, goat's:
  grilled goat's cheese on
    country bread, 50
  pizzas, 45
cheese, soft:
  black mushroom roulade, 107
  cheese and herb creams, 26
  quenelles, 18
  spanakopitta, 39
  tiramisu, 147
  vegetable lasagne, 118-19
chestnuts, glazed, 76
Chez Panisse, Berkeley, 14, 32,
    54
chick peas:
  chick pea and vegetable
    salad, 69
  hummus, 44
  root vegetable and chick pea
    curry, 93
chicory, braised, 84
Chinese leaves:
  steamed Chinese leaves and
    mangetout, 77
  stir-fried greens with
    preserved ginger and
    sesame seeds, 79
choux pastry, 38
Christmas dinner menu, 166
cider:
  artichoke and asparagus
    casserole in butter and
    cider sauce, 28

cider bread, 153
Clark, Sheila, 146
coconut milk, 95
coffee:
  tiramisu, 147
Coleslaw, 66-7
Colettes, Beverly Hills, 13
Connaught Hotel, London, 54
cookies, pumpkin seed, 159
corn:
  aubergine, corn and tomato
    soup, 13
cornbread, 156
cornmeal *see* polenta
courgettes:
  chilled courgette and potato
    soup
  courgette and herb risotto,
    127
  courgette flan, 133
  Gruyère and courgette batter
    pudding, 51
  pisto Manchego, 49
  ratatouille, 102-3
  vegetable lasagne, 118-19
  warm leek and courgette
    salad, 69
court bouillon, 30
couscous:
  couscous salad, 68
  vegetable couscous, 104
creams, chilled persimmon, 139
crumbles:
  celeriac, pumpkin and
    walnut, 94
pear and blackberry, 140
  ratatouille, 103
  wild greens and wild rice, 99
cucumber:

cucumber and mint salad, 64-5
  salad Elona, 65
  stewed cucumbers, 78
cumin pastry, *dhal* tart with,
    130
curries:
  aubergine and okra brown,
    95
  garden, 96
  mild curried potato omelette,
    48-9
  root vegetable and chick pea,
    93
custard sauce, 120
desserts, 137-47
dhal, 84
dhal tart with cumin pastry, 130
dips:
  hummus, 44
  vegetables with dips, 26-7
dressings, 60
  herb, walnut and lemon, 27
  pinziminio, 27
  raspberry, 64
  salad cream, 66-7
  tomato and basil vinaigrette,
    29
  warm garlic and pinenut
    cream, 72
dried fruit:
  fruit and nut bread, 151
  fruit and nut casserole, 139
  wholemeal fruit and nut
    biscuits, American style,
    158-9
  winter pudding, 141

eggs, 7
  asparagus and potato

omelette, 47
  eggs casho, 48
  frittata of wild greens, 46
  mild curried potato omelette,
    48-9
  pipérade, 47
  pisto Manchego, 49
  poached eggs in field
    mushrooms, 45
  Spanish omelette, 135
entertaining, 163-7

farmhouse cheese pie, 134
feast menu, 167
fennel:
  fennel and pomegranate
    salad, 61
  fennel with cheese sauce, 30-1
flans, savoury *see* tarts, savoury
flour, 7
  bread-making, 148
fondue, cheese, 132
fonduta, 50
frittata of wild greens, 46
fruit *see* dried fruit *and*
    individual types of fruit
fusilli tricolore, 122

galettes, buckwheat, 57
garden curry, 96
garlic:
  dried tomato and garlic soup,
    21
  grilled aubergine, onion and
    pepper salad with warm
    garlic and pinenut cream, 72
  patatas alioli, 77
  roast new potatoes and garlic,
    80

roasted garlic, Gorgonzola
    and toasted pinenuts, 43
  warm green bean, garlic and
    potato salad, 71
ginger:
  ginger mousse with lime and
    honey sauce, 143
  stir-fried greens with
    preserved ginger and
    sesame seeds, 79
Glamorgan sausages, 133
globe artichokes *see* artichokes
gluten, 148
gnocchi, potato, 123
goat's cheese *see* cheese, goat's
golden bread, 151
gougère, 38
Grahame, Peter, 63
grains, 129-31
Grant, Doris, 154
Grant loaf, 154-5
grapes:
  muscat grape tart with
    melted butter pastry, 146
gratin, winter vegetable, 101
green beans:
  fusilli tricolore, 122
  spaghetti Genoese style, 115
  warm green bean, garlic and
    potato salad, 71
greens:
  frittata of wild greens, 46
  stir-fried greens with
    preserved ginger and
    sesame seeds, 79
  wild greens and barley
    'risotto', 98
  wild greens and wild rice
    crumble, 99

Gruyère and courgette batter
    pudding, 51
gumbo, vegetable, 20

hazelnut sauce, 113
herbs:
  cheese and herb creams, 26
  herb and Gorgonzola sauce,
    114
  herb bread, 151
  herb butter, 114
  herb, walnut and lemon
    dressing, 27
honey:
  ginger mousse with lime and
    honey sauce, 143
  honey-glazed Stilton
    potatoes, 90
hot sauce, 104
hummus, 44
ice cream:
  banana and rum tofu, 142
  quick banana and cardamom,
    145
ingredients, 6-7
  bread-making, 148-9, 150-1
InterContinental Hotel,
    London, 53
Italian menu, 167

Jerusalem artichokes, baked, 76

kneading bread, 149
knocking back bread, 149
Kromberg, Peter, 53, 54

La Choza, Quito, 40
Lancelloti family, 64
lasagne, vegetable, 118-19

leeks:
  creamed leeks, 79
  deep-fried leeks, 78
  leek, potato and Parmesan
    strudel, 100
  vegetable lasagne, 118-19
  warm leek and courgette
    salad, 69
lemon:
  herb, walnut and lemon
    dressing, 27
  homemade lemon pasta, 112
  lemon-glazed carrots, 74
  lemon sauce, 114
  tagliolini al limone, 117
lentils:
  dhal, 84
  dhal tart with cumin pastry,
    130
  lentil salad, 62
  quinoa and lentil strudel, 131
lettuce:
  broad beans and peas with
    cream and lettuce, 74
Licciardi, Emilio, 117
light meals and snacks, 35-57
lime:
  celeriac with lime, 75
  ginger mousse with lime and
    honey sauce, 143
llapingachos, 40
lunch menu, 165

main dishes, 87-135
mangetout, steamed Chinese
  leaves and, 77
marinated carrot salad, 61
marinated mushrooms, 81
marmalade:

lemon-glazed carrots, 74
orange bread, 151
quire of orange pancakes
  with marmalade sauce,
  142-3
melted butter pastry, 146
menus, 165-7
minestrone, 19
mint:
  broccoli, broad bean and
    mint risotto, 125
  cucumber and mint salad,
    64-5
  mint sambol, 85
mixed grain and seed bread,
  154
mostarda di Cremona, 111
mostarda di frutta, 111
mousses:
  ginger mousse with lime and
    honey sauce, 143
  Stilton mousse, 34
muscat grape tart with melted
  butter pastry, 146
mushrooms:
  black mushroom roulade, 107
  cabbage stuffed with wild
    mushrooms, 92
  creamy cep polenta, 129
  eggs casho, 48
  fried puffballs, 80
  fusilli tricolore, 122
  grilled polenta slices with
    mushrooms, 42
  marinated mushrooms, 81
  mushroom and red wine
    risotto, 126-7
  mushroom salad, 62
  poached eggs in field

mushrooms, 45
  potato and wild mushroom
    salad, 68
  radishes with three butters, 44
  spaghetti alla Norcina, 116
nasturtium flowers:
  golden bread, 151
nuts:
  fruit and nut bread, 151
  fruit and nut casserole, 139
  wholemeal fruit and nut
    biscuits, American style,
    158-9
  see also individual types of nuts

oatmeal:
  mixed grain and seed bread,
    154
  oatmeal soda bread, 155
Ogden, Bradley, 129
okra:
  aubergine and okra brown
    curry, 95
  aubergine, okra and tomato
    stew, 91
  vegetable gumbo, 20
olive oil, 60
  patatas alioli, 77
olives:
  olive bread, 151
  orange, onion and olive salad, 63
omelettes:
  asparagus and potato, 47
  mild curried potato, 48-9
  Spanish, 135
onions:
  grilled aubergine, onion and
    pepper salad with warm
    garlic and pinenut cream, 72

onion and cheese soup under a
    soufflé, 22-3
  onion bread, 150
  onion salad, 63
  onion soup, 23
  onions in red wine, 75
  orange, onion and olive salad,
    63
  ratatouille, 102-3
oranges:
  orange bread, 151
  orange, onion and olive salad,
    63
  quire of orange pancakes
    with marmalade sauce,
    142-3
pancakes, 56-7
  asparagus terrine, 105
  buckwheat galettes, 57
  potato pancakes, 40
  quire of orange pancakes
    with marmalade sauce,
    142-3
parsnips:
  spiced carrot and parsnip
    soup, 14
pasta, 110-22
  homemade lemon pasta, 112
  pasta with broccoli, chives
    and blue cheese, 119
  rich vegetable and pasta pie,
    120-1
  simple pasta sauces, 113-14
  tagliolini al limone, 117
  *see also individual types of
    pasta*
pastries, cheese and asparagus,
  41
pastry:

choux, 38
  cumin, 130
  melted butter, 146
patatas alioli, 77
Paterson, Jennifer, 109
peaches:
  carrot and peach soup, 24
pears:
  pear and blackberry crumble,
    140
  pear and herb salad with
    raspberry dressing, 64
peas:
  broad beans and peas with
    cream and lettuce, 74
  pea and herb soup, 12
  salad of peas and beans, 66
peppers:
  aubergine and red pepper
    terrine, 106
  grilled aubergine, onion and
    pepper salad with warm
    garlic and pinenut cream,
    72
  grilled or roasted pepper
    salad, 65
  pipérade, 47
  pisto Manchego, 49
  ratatouille, 102-3
persimmon creams, chilled, 139
pies:
  asparagus and almonds in
    filo, 89
  farmhouse cheese pie, 134
  leek, potato and Parmesan
    strudel, 100
  quinoa and lentil strudel, 131
  rich vegetable and pasta pie,
    120-1

spanakopitta, 39
  see also crumbles
pineapple and rum soufflés, 144
pinenuts:
  grilled aubergine, onion and
    pepper salad with warm
    garlic and pinenut cream,
    72
  roasted garlic, Gorgonzola
    and toasted pinenuts, 43
pinziminio, 37
pipérade, 47
pisto Manchego, 49
pizzas, 45
planning meals, 164
poached and marinated
    vegetables, 30
polenta:
  cornbread, 156
  creamy cep polenta, 129
  grilled polenta slices with
    mushrooms, 42-3
pomegranates:
  fennel and pomegranate
    salad, 61
potatoes:
  aligot, 82-3
  aloo gobi subji, 83
  artichoke and potato
    casserole, 90-1
  asparagus and potato
    omelette, 47
  boxty, 157
  chilled courgette and potato
    soup, 25
  honey-glazed Stilton
    potatoes, 90
leek, potato and Parmesan
    strudel, 100

llapingachos, 40
mild curried potato omelette, 48-9
mushroom and potato pie, 97
patatas alioli, 77
potato and wild mushroom salad, 68
potato gnocchi, 123
potato pancakes, 40
potato scones, 157
roast new potatoes and garlic, 80
spaghetti Genoese style, 115
Spanish omelette, 135
summer vichyssoise, 24-5
warm green bean, garlic and potato salad, 71
potted cheese, 31
profiteroles, Roquefort, 52
proving bread, 149
puffballs, fried, 80
pulses, 129-31
soaking and cooking, 7
pumpkin:
celeriac, pumpkin and walnut crumble, 94
pumpkin and almond soup, 17
pumpkin ravioli, 110-11
pumpkin risotto, 126
pumpkin seeds:
mixed grain and seed bread, 154
pumpkin seed cookies, 159

quenelles, 18
quinoa and lentil strudel, 131
quire of orange pancakes with marmalade sauce, 142-3

radicchio:
grilled radicchio, 82
radicchio and Parmesan salad, 70
radishes with three butters, 44
rarebit, traditional baked, 52
raspberry dressing, pear and herb salad with, 64
ratatouille, 102-3
ratatouille crumble, 103
ravioli, pumpkin, 110-11
red cabbage:
spiced red cabbage, 73
see also cabbage
rice:
basmati rice, 85
see also risotto; wild rice
risotto, 124
asparagus, 128
broccoli, broad bean and mint, 125
courgette and herb, 127
mushroom and red wine, 126-7
pumpkin, 126
risotto nero al balsamico, 125
wild greens and barley 'risotto', 98
Roman-style artichokes, 33
root vegetables:
root vegetable and chick pea curry, 93
white root salad, 70
Roquefort profiteroles, 52
roulade, black mushroom, 107
rum:
banana and rum tofu ice cream, 142

pineapple and rum soufflés, 144

saffron:
quick saffron bread, 156
saffron bread, 151
salad cream, 66-7
salads, 59-72
aubergine, 46
bread and tomato, 71
chick pea and vegetable, 69
coleslaw, 66-7
couscous, 68
cucumber and mint, 64-5
fennel and pomegranate, 61
grilled aubergine, onion and pepper, 72
grilled or roasted pepper, 64
lentil, 62
marinated carrot, 61
mushroom, 62
onion, 63
orange, onion and olive, 63
pear and herb with raspberry dressing, 64
potato and wild mushroom, 68
radicchio and Parmesan, 70
salad Elona, 65
salad of peas and beans, 66
salade Huguette, 67
warm green bean, garlic and potato, 71
warm leek and courgette, 69
white root, 70
salt, bread-making, 148
sambol, mint, 85
sauces:
béchamel, 118

celery and sun-dried tomato, 113
custard, 120
hazelnut, 113
herb and Gorgonzola, 114
hot, 104
lemon, 114
lime and honey, 143
marmalade, 142-3
mushroom, 42
simple pasta sauces, 113-14
with soufflés, 55
tomato, 118, 120
yellow tomato, 114
sausages, Glamorgan, 133
scones:
potato, 157
teatime, 158
wholemeal fruit and nut biscuits, American style, 158-9
seed bread, 151
sesame seeds:
stir-fried greens with preserved ginger and sesame seeds, 79
stir-fried vegetables and toasted sesame tartlets, 37
side dishes, 60, 73-86
snacks, 35-37
soda bread, oatmeal, 155
soufflés, 53-5
basic savoury soufflés, 54
cheese soufflés in paper cases, 55
onion and cheese soup under a soufflé, 22-3
pineapple and rum soufflés, 144

sauces with, 55
savoury soufflé variations, 54
soups, 9-25
asparagus, 12-13
asparagus and almond, 16
aubergine, corn and tomato, 13
beetroot and tomato, 21
black bean, 15
carrot and peach, 24
chilled courgette and potato, 25
cream of spinach, 16-17
dried tomato and garlic, 21
fresh tomato soup with quenelles, 18
minestrone, 19
onion, 23
onion and cheese soup under a soufflé, 22-3
pea and herb, 12
pumpkin and almond, 17
spiced carrot and parsnip, 14
summer vichyssoise, 24-5
vegetable broth, 11
vegetable gumbo, 20
watercress, 22
soy sauce:
broccoli with tomato and soy butter, 32
spaghetti:
spaghetti alla Norcina, 116
spaghetti Genoese style, 115
spaghetti with uncooked tomato sauce, 115
spanakopitta, 39
Spanish omelette, 135
spiced carrot and parsnip soup, 14

spiced red cabbage, 73
spinach:
cream of spinach soup, 16-17
spanakopitta, 39
Spanish omelette, 135
stir-fried greens with preserved ginger and sesame seeds, 79
starters, 26-34
stews *see* casseroles and stews; curries
Stilton mousse, 34
stocks, 10
straccia denti, 162
strawberries:
salad Elona, 65
strudels:
leek, potato and Parmesan, 100
quinoa and lentil, 131
summer lunch menu, 165
summer vichyssoise, 24-5
sunflower seeds:
mixed grain and seed bread, 154
supper menus, 165, 166
sweet and sour cabbage, 73

tagliolini al limone, 117
tarts, savoury:
courgette flan, 133
dhal tart with cumin pastry, 130
stir-fried vegetables and toasted sesame tartlets, 37
tomato tart, 108
tarts, sweet:
muscat grape tart with melted butter pastry, 146
teatime scones, 158

terrines:
  asparagus, 105
  aubergine and red pepper,
    106
testing for 'doneness', bread,
  150
Texas 'caviar', 130-1
tiramisu, 147
tofu:
  banana and rum tofu ice
    cream, 142
  vegetable and tofu creams, 29
tomatoes:
  aubergine, corn and tomato
    soup, 13
  aubergine, okra and tomato
    stew, 91
  beetroot and tomato soup, 21
  bread and tomato salad, 71
  broccoli with tomato and soy
    butter, 32
  celery and sun-dried tomato
    sauce, 113
  dried tomato and garlic soup,
    21
  fresh tomato soup with
    quenelles, 18
  fusilli tricolore, 122
  pipérade, 47
  pisto Manchego, 49
  pizzas, 45
  radishes with three butters,
    44
  ratatouille, 102-3
  spaghetti with uncooked
    tomato sauce, 115
  tomato and basil vinaigrette,
    29
  tomato bread, 150

tomato puddings, 109
tomato sauce, 118, 120
tomato tart, 108
yellow tomato sauce, 114
traditional baked rarebit, 52
truffles:
  spaghetti alla Norcina, 116
turnips, creamed, 81

Van den Hurk, Ida, 34
vegetables:
  golden curry, 96
  poached and marinated
    vegetables, 30
  ratatouille, 102-3
  rich vegetable and pasta pie,
    120-1
  side dishes, 60, 73-86
  stir-fried vegetables and
    toasted sesame tartlets, 37
  summer vichyssoise, 24-5
  vegetable and tofu creams, 29
  vegetable broth, 11
  vegetable couscous, 104
  vegetable gumbo, 20
  vegetable lasagne, 118-19
  vegetables with dips, 26-7
  winter vegetable gratin, 101
  see also salads *and individual
    types of vegetable*
vegetarian feast menu, 167
Verucci, Franco, 117
vichyssoise, summer, 24-5
vinaigrette, tomato and basil, 29
vinegar, 60
walnuts:
  celeriac, pumpkin and walnut
    crumble, 94
  herb, walnut and lemon

  dressing, 27
water, in bread-making, 149
watercress:
  radishes with three butters,
    44
  watercress soup, 22
Waters, Alice, 14, 43, 54
white root salad, 70
wholemeal fruit and nut
    biscuits, American style,
    158-9
wild greens *see* greens
wild rice:
  wild greens and wild rice
    crumble, 99
wine:
  biscotti di vino, 161
  mushroom and red wine
    risotto, 126-7
  onions in red wine, 75
winter menu, 165
winter pudding, 141
winter vegetable gratin, 101

Yates, Caroline, 107
yeast, 148
yellow tomato sauce, 114